CITY BY DESIGN

an architectural perspective of chicago

Published by

PANACHE
P A N A C H E   P A R T N E R S

Panache Partners, LLC
1424 Gables Court
Plano, Texas 75075
469.246.6060
Fax: 469.246.6062
www.panache.com

Publishers: Brian G. Carabet and John A. Shand

Printed in Malaysia

Distributed by Independent Publishers Group
800.888.4741

PUBLISHER'S DATA

City by Design Chicago
Library of Congress Control Number: 2008920697

ISBN 13: 978-1-933415-51-2
ISBN 10: 1-933415-51-7

First Printing 2008

10 9 8 7 6 5 4 3 2

Previous Page: 111 South Wacker, Goettsch Partners, page 246
Photograph by James Steinkamp Photography

Right: Navy Pier, VOA Associates, Inc., BTA Benjamin Thompson & Associates, page 48
Photograph by Vito Palmisano

CITY BY DESIGN

an architectural perspective of chicago

FOREWORD

by Stanley Tigerman, FAIA

The work presented in this book is significantly different than work that might have been gathered in 1998, 1988 or 1978 in that any earlier version might have conformed to an overarching stylistic—or even constructional/structural—métier. But in 2008, multivalence seems to have overtaken design representations. In an earlier time, the tall building would have generally conformed to "Chicago School" antecedents, but not today, when the expression of structure and formal expressions are equally influential in informing design. This is not to suggest value in earlier or current epochs—it is simply fact. The many forces that now influence a building's form produce a lively skyline unheard of in earlier eras. While, as always, quality is all over the lot, one can no longer accuse Chicago architects of being one-dimensional in their approach to design. Each of us brings our own values to discussions like this. The projects I've chosen to digress about represent divergent ways of working through building programs, unique sites and the like.

A few of the featured large-scale residential projects are conventional—commissioned by developers—though the results are anything but market driven. Ralph Johnson of Perkins + Will has produced a mid-rise condominium complex harkening back not to Mies as common denominator but to Le Corbusier as antecedent. Lucien Lagrange's Erie on the Park is equally sculpturally expressive but presented in an entirely different way. Lucien and his staff have used an exposed-steel structure—including diagonal bracing—to contain high-rise dwelling units without synthesizing the overall form. While the building in some ways reflects a Miesian influence, its energetic way of expressing itself is anything but Miesian. Studio Gang's 80-story Aqua high rise, while apparently idiosyncratic, is well within Chicago's structurally expressive tradition. The base building is almost boringly normative, but the out-of-sync balconies produce a compelling image that is one-of-a-kind in Chicago building lore. David Hovey's Optima Old Orchard Woods is a brilliant addition to Chicago's reservoir of residential buildings, but what is truly unique is that his firm designs, engineers, builds and sells its projects. David Hovey as master builder is the only one of his kind who never seems to compromise architecture. David has somehow managed to bring Mies and Le Corbusier together in this project that persuasively presents the result as a natural amalgam.

Three of the commercial office projects represent large-scale Central Business District designs that have a major impact on both the skyline and animated use. The first and by far the largest of these projects is Trump Tower by Skidmore, Owings & Merrill. The building's façade is beautifully detailed and is far more elegant than any prior tower named on behalf of its developer, and as such is a credit to the architects' power of persuasion. Goettsch Partners' 111 South Wacker is noted for its transparent ground-floor lobby—not all office building lobbies

Contemporaine, Perkins + Will, page 94

Peggy Notebaert Nature Museum, Perkins + Will, page 174

are as welcoming and this project should be perceived as a role model. The mixed-use Block 37 project—still in progress—is in the heart of The Loop. Its notorious site has been the repository of design efforts over many years and was once the subject of a book. The lead architect, Gensler, is the world's largest design firm and has a history of producing competent, if not always brilliant, efforts on commercial ventures and this one seems to be heading in that direction.

In the realm of institutional projects, the Peggy Notebaert Nature Museum by Ralph Johnson and the Spertus Institute by Krueck and Sexton are particularly noteworthy: the former because of its debt to Frank Lloyd Wright, the latter simply by virtue of its quality. The nature museum is very much a part of its park-like setting, while the Spertus Institute responds innovatively to—and subtly plays off of—its share in the wall of buildings that defines Michigan Avenue.

The addition to the existing Soldier Field stadium by Wood + Zapata and Lohan Caprile Goettsch Architects was controversial from the start, though there is no denying the energy that it brings to the city. On the other hand, Millenium Park—although over budget and four years late—is a huge success with tourists and a major profit center for the city. Frank Gehry's Jay Pritzker Pavilion and the snake-like bridge represent tour de force elements that animate the park. *Cloud Gate* and *Crown Fountain* are wildly popular, and both help to make the entire gathering place an urban success.

City by Design Chicago helps to explain the sense of energy currently animating our city and present paradigms that other cities could find useful as they attempt to energize their own urban contexts.

Soldier Field and North Burnham Park Redevelopment,
Wood + Zapata, Lohan Caprile Goettsch Architects, page 56

The Spertus Institute of Jewish Studies,
Krueck & Sexton Architects, page128

The Heritage at Millennium Park, Mesa Development, LLC,
Walsh Investors, LLC, page 106

INTRODUCTION

Each day we pass by hundreds of buildings—a mélange of old and new works of architecture—that we likely take for granted, not for lack of interest but because life's frenetic pace often prohibits asking why, how, when and through whose creativity did the built environment around us come to fruition. Yet it is these very structures, unassuming or prominently placed, that create the brilliantly complex urban and suburban landscapes where our lives unfold.

Imagine being afforded the rare opportunity to gaze inside the walls and around the perimeter of these buildings that are equal parts mysterious, familiar and alluring. Imagine meeting their creators and discovering the forward-thinking design savvy behind the selection of each material, the placement of each door and window, the sculptural use of both classical and contemporary architectural forms. Now turn the page—commence an invigorating journey that is sure to ignite your appreciation or renew your passion for Chicago's architectural fabric.

You will immediately discern *City by Design Chicago* as unique among architectural collections. Indeed, it boasts vibrant photographs of stimulating designs, melded with insightful editorial, yet it does not endeavor to present merely the tallest, widest, newest, oldest or greenest buildings. More precisely, it is a rich, diverse collection of the city's best—from landmark skyscrapers that define Chicago's majestic skyline to smaller, thoughtfully designed edifices of some of the suburbs' best-kept secrets. It is a regional compilation of masterfully conceived structures considered preeminent by the locally based architects and developers who have turned intangible ideas into built realities that will be enjoyed for generations to come.

455 North Park Drive Hotel and Residences, Fordham Company, page 276

Trump International Hotel & Tower Chicago, Skidmore, Owings & Merrill LLP, page 304

CONTENTS

CHAPTER ONE – BUILT TO PLAY AND STAY

Millennium Park 14
City of Chicago
Millennium Park, Inc.

Alhambra Palace 20
Absolute Architecture PC

Beyond the Ivy 24
Kutleša + Hernandez Architects, Inc.

The Blackstone Hotel 28
Lucien Lagrange Architects

Garmin International Flagship Store 32
Valerio Dewalt Train Associates

Luxbar 36
Shapiro Associates

Makray Memorial Golf Clubhouse 40
Gillespie Design Group

Meadows Club 44
Arzoumanian & Company

Navy Pier 48
VOA Associates, Incorporated
BTA Benjamin Thompson & Associates

Ping Tom Memorial Park 52
Site Design Group, Ltd.

Soldier Field
and North Burnham Park Redevelopment 56
Wood + Zapata
Lohan Caprile Goettsch Architects

Superdawg 60
Shapiro Associates

Woodlands at the Promenade 64
Techcon Dallas, Inc.

CHAPTER TWO – URBAN LIVING

Optima Old Orchard Woods 70
David Hovey, FAIA Architect, Optima, Inc.

160 East Illinois Street 78
Built Form, LLC

5350 South Shore Drive 82
Nicholas Clark Architects, Ltd.

65 East Goethe 86
Fordham Company

Club 2700 90
Myefski Cook Architects

Contemporaine 94
Perkins + Will

Erie on the Park 98
Lucien Lagrange Architects

The Fordham 102
Fordham Company

The Heritage at Millennium Park 106
Mesa Development, LLC
Walsh Investors, LLC

Lakeshore East 110
Loewenberg Architects, LLC

Park Tower 114
Lucien Lagrange Architects

River Village Pointe 118
Hirsch Associates LLC

Vetro 122
Roszak/ADC

CHAPTER THREE – CITY PROJECTS

The Spertus Institute of Jewish Studies 128
Krueck & Sexton Architects

850 Lake Shore Drive 134
Integrated Development Group
Booth Hansen
Interior Design Associates

ABLA/Fosco Community Center 138
Nia Architects, Inc.

Armenian Evangelical Church of Chicago. 142
Arzoumanian & Company

Bloomingdale's and Tree Studios 146
Daniel P. Coffey & Associates, Ltd.

Christian Life Center 150
McBride Kelley Baurer

Evanston Fire Station #3 154
Yas Architecture, LLC

Grace Church 158
Ethos Workshop

Museum of Science and Industry
U-505 Submarine Exhibit 162
Goettsch Partners

Oriental Theatre. 166
Daniel P. Coffey & Associates, Ltd.

The Park at Lakeshore East. 170
Site Design Group, Ltd.

Peggy Notebaert Nature Museum 174
Perkins + Will

Sullivan Center 178
Joseph Freed and Associates LLC

Willow Creek Community Church 182
Goss Pasma Blomquist Architects

Wrigley Building 186
Powell/Kleinschmidt, Inc.
David Zeunert & Associates, Inc.

CHAPTER FOUR – INDUSTRY LEADERS

Access Living 192
LCM Architects

Kennedy-King College 198
Johnson & Lee Architects/Planners, Ltd.
VOA Associates, Incorporated

McCormick Place Convention Center 204
TVS Design

University of Illinois at Chicago
Student Recreation Facility. 210
PSA-Dewberry

1363 Shermer 216
Myefski Cook Architects

Advocate Lutheran General Hospital
Center for Advanced Care 220
OWP/P

Marianjoy Rehabilitation Hospital 224
Stephen Rankin Associates

Naperville Public Library
95th Street Facility 228
PSA-Dewberry

Second Federal Savings 232
W. Steven Gross / Architectural Associates

United Auto Workers Region 4 Headquarters 236
The Hezner Corporation

Walter Payton College Preparatory High School 240
DeStefano and Partners

CHAPTER FIVE – SUSTAINING GROWTH

111 South Wacker. 246
Goettsch Partners

340 on the Park 250
Solomon Cordwell Buenz

Exelon Corporation Corporate Headquarters 254
Epstein

Harm A. Weber Academic Center 258
Burnidge Cassell Associates

The Merchandise Mart 262
Merchandise Mart Properties, Inc.

Tuthill Corporate Headquarters 266
Serena Sturm Architects, Ltd.

Vernon Hills Village Hall 270
Yas Architecture, LLC

CHAPTER SIX – CITY FUTURES

455 North Park Drive Hotel and Residences 276
Fordham Company

Block 37 280
Joseph Freed and Associates LLC

The Legacy at Millennium Park 284
Mesa Development, LLC
Walsh Investors, LLC

Mandarin Oriental, Chicago 288
Solomon Cordwell Buenz

PURE. 292
Weiss Architects, LLC

Schaumburg Center for the Performing Arts 296
Daniel P. Coffey & Associates, Ltd.

Solstice on the Park. 300
Antheus Capital, LLC
Studio Gang Architects

Trump International Hotel & Tower Chicago 304
Skidmore, Owings & Merrill LLP

Vista Luxury Condominiums 308
Arzoumanian & Company

X|O .312
Lucien Lagrange Architects

CHAPTER ONE
Built to Play and Stay

From early morning to afternoon, evening and night, the city swirls about with activity. At the heart of this vibrant energy are its retail, hospitality, dining and recreation establishments, be they classically inspired structures, crisp displays of modern architecture or a happy medium between the two.

Whether exploring the wonders of Alhambra Palace by Absolute Architecture, enjoying the outdoors in Ping Tom Memorial Park by Site Design Group, or having fun at Navy Pier by VOA Associates and BTA, numerous recreation options exist throughout the streets of downtown and neighboring suburbs.

The savviest of boutique-company entrepreneurs recognize and appreciate the value in working with architects to define their style and present a prominent image to the world, while the masterminds behind nationally run entities have already witnessed, firsthand, the power of carefully crafted architecture. The designs of these engaging and, at times, whimsical venues showcase the innovative nature of their architects.

The Blackstone Hotel, Lucien Lagrange Architects, page 28

Millennium Park, City of Chicago, Millennium Park, Inc., page 14

Garmin International Flagship Store, Valerio Dewalt Train Associates, page 32

Millennium Park

■ ■

City of Chicago
Millennium Park, Inc.

■ ■ ■ ■ ■ ■ ■ ■ ■ ■ ■ If there is a Chicago place that reaches a worldwide audience, it is Millennium Park. The universal appeal of this lakefront cultural

venue is astounding, for even its opening weekend drew in a reported 300,000 people. This must-see destination houses some of Chicago's most fascinating

structures and, thanks to Ed Uhlir who was the project design director for the City of Chicago, earns its moniker, for it truly is a place of the new millennium.

With multiple visions within landscaped rooms, Millennium Park forms a single concept to give to the city a great common space.

Opened in 2004, Millennium Park came not without its obstacles, for its initial design had some significant problems. One, it did not follow the principles of

universal design, which allows barrier-free access for all. Two, the park design extended over an existing parking garage that ultimately would need to

ABOVE: Millennium Park was destined for greatness at its 2004 opening.
Photograph by City of Chicago/Chris McGuire

FACING PAGE: Frank Gehry's Jay Pritzker Pavilion offers an innovative concert experience.
Photograph by City of Chicago/Chris McGuire

be rebuilt. And three, the initial design did not propel architecture into the next millennium—it was too historical, with no enthusiasm for the future. Millennium Park, Inc., the Blue Ribbon Committee and the mayor of Chicago wanted the best in the world. Rebuilding the existing parking garage and adding a new underground garage provided the platform to create this 24.5-acre park, upon which world-renowned architects and artists could propel the park into the 21st century.

Under constant press scrutiny, the Millennium Park project was a very public affair—a 475-million-dollar development tends to do that. But with the support of Mayor Daley, almost 50 percent of the budget was raised from private donors led by John Bryan, the CEO of Sara Lee at the time. This philanthropic effort changed the dynamic of the park.

One of the most recognizable features of Millennium Park is *Cloud Gate*. Designed by Anish Kapoor, this 110-ton, 66-foot-long, stainless-steel object, affectionately called "The Bean," reflects the sky, the skyline and anybody who happens to be standing anywhere near it. No less attention-getting are Frank Gehry's Jay Pritzker Pavilion and BP Bridge. The Pavilion is one of the most

TOP LEFT: Designed by Anish Kapoor, the bean-like *Cloud Gate* playfully offsets strong Chicagoan structures.
Photograph by City of Chicago/Walter Mitchell

BOTTOM LEFT: Summer heat advisories draw everyone to the interactive *Crown Fountain*.
Photograph by City of Chicago

FACING PAGE: The modernity of Gehry's Jay Pritzker Pavilion mixes with the tranquility of Lurie Garden.
Photograph by Mark Tomaras

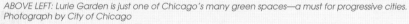

ABOVE LEFT: Lurie Garden is just one of Chicago's many green spaces—a must for progressive cities.
Photograph by City of Chicago

ABOVE RIGHT: The serpentine BP Bridge is Gehry's first pedestrian bridge.
Photograph by Howard Ash

FACING PAGE: The Bean, as Cloud Gate is also known, is one of the most photographed attractions in the world.
Photograph by City of Chicago/Patrick Pyszka

high-tech outdoor music venues in the world, with a trellis network that extends outward from the stage, which supports its incredible sound system—a Gehry invention. The BP Bridge is Gehry's first executed pedestrian span. This 925-foot serpentine bridge not only defers traffic noise from the lawn but also has a five-percent slope for easy crossing. Likewise, *Crown Fountain*, by Jaume Plensa, has a shallow reflecting pool with two, 50-foot glass block towers, and the digital faces of 1,000 Chicagoans who send squirts of water down to those below.

Since the park's opening, Ed Uhlir has found himself coordinating additional improvements to the park, as well as giving lectures on public works projects. In any territory where millions of people show up, keeping an eye out for betterments is of high priority. As we head into the new millennium, Chicago can feel comfort knowing that it is leading the way. ■ ■ ■ ■ ■ ■ ■ ■ ■ ■ ■

Alhambra Palace

■ ■

Absolute Architecture PC

■ ■ ■ ■ ■ ■ ■ ■ ■ ■ The Arabic culture has long been famous for its unique form of hospitality—feasts served while belly dancers whirl to exotic music against a backdrop of hypnotizing, ornate architecture. In Chicago, a recent addition to the often underrepresented Arabic culture is Alhambra Palace, a restaurant, banquet and cabaret, with a 1,000-person occupancy, that is an explosion of commingled Middle Eastern traditions that trace back 5,000 years. Named after a Spanish castle and palace built by the Moors at a high point of Arabic civilization, Alhambra Palace is an authentic, massive, Arabic oasis for anyone interested in an evening out of the ordinary.

From the start, the owner, Dr. Naser Rustom, and the architect, James A. Kapche, AIA, agreed that the key element of the design was to be authenticity. Reproductions made in the United States just would not do. On a tour of Spain, North Africa and the Middle East, Alhambra Palace's owner bought

FACING PAGE: The two-story cabaret features a traditional inlaid wood floor, designed with cherry, maple and black walnut. All of the detailing, furniture and finishes are authentic.
Project Design Team: James A. Kapche, Warren Gary, Taylor Cline and Joe Signorelli.
Photograph by Robert Bonicoro

and shipped enough representative artwork to fill some 60 containers. The sorting began. One of the key features of Arabic art is elaborate, interweaving mathematical patterns. All surfaces, furniture and fixtures in Alhambra Palace contain traditional Arabic pattern motifs representing cultures stretching from Spain across North Africa and through Mesopotamia. The elements produced in the United States, such as the main dining room floor, also feature these weaving patterns, centralizing at a 12-sided star inset with natural woods: cherry, black walnut and maple. The stone mosaic floor tile patterns—containing more than 10,000 tiles each—were so complicated that they were shipped in preformed inlaid panels.

Finding the perfect location for such a huge venue required a little patience. The actual site of Alhambra Palace is the third purchased, after the owner recognized that the potential to draw huge crowds—while making a lot of noise—required a location receptive to a late-night scene. West Randolph Street in Chicago has become nightclub row with one venue after another offering a unique culinary and entertainment experience. The street comes alive at dark, which is great for Alhambra Palace, for the adventure begins at dusk—music, belly dancers and a mixture of Middle Eastern and French food. This 30,000-square-foot building was originally a one-story warehouse, but the Absolute Architecture team popped the top and added a second floor to house the banquet hall and to allow the cabaret two stories of cross-cultural amusement.

TOP LEFT: The entrance features two onion domes with traditional Middle Eastern dimensions, as well as the name in English and Arabic.
Photograph by Robert Bonicoro

BOTTOM LEFT: The main lounge area features mosaic floor patterns, marble columns, ceiling medallions and light fixtures handmade in Syria and Spain.
Photograph by Robert Bonicoro

FACING PAGE: The lounge is highlighted by the hand-carved cornice mouldings, mosaic tile wall hangings and wrought-iron lounge seating all handmade in Syria.
Photograph by Robert Bonicoro

So Alhambra beckons. Come and enjoy. For a moment leave Chicago and travel to the other side of the world to the cradle of western civilization. It is easy to forget how much of our own culture comes from the Middle East. All modern architecture, mathematics and music started in the culture that Alhambra represents. With the ancient yet visually stimulating architecture, Alhambra Palace has foods that are a rich sampling of Arabic tradition—baba ghanoush, tangine and baklava are ever popular, especially complemented by dhoog. But the experience is certainly not restricted to those who reside in the Middle East. Try it—for the only thing that could distract you from the mesmerizing architecture may be the belly dancer. ■ ■ ■ ■ ■ ■ ■ ■ ■ ■ ■

Beyond the Ivy

■ ■

Kutleša + Hernandez Architects, Inc.

■ ■ ■ ■ ■ ■ ■ ■ ■ ■ Welcome to Wrigleyville, home of the second-oldest Major League Baseball field, and also one of the smallest. Wrigley Field has low outfield bleachers and has always had the fortune of a close proximity to tall brownstones, which, in times past, allowed for economical, non-stadium seating of the lawn chair sort; people wanted to experience the game without the exorbitant pricing. And, frankly, the too-few stadium seats were frequently sold-out. In the 1990s, the owners of these adjacent buildings struck a financial deal with Wrigley Field to add bleachers to the rooftops, and the result was Beyond the Ivy.

Commissioned for the construction of the bleacher addition was Kutleša + Hernandez Architects. As Wrigley expanded up and out about 20 feet higher, the bleachers needed to be massive structures that would function as premier rooftop spots for networking and other business settings; a good Cubs game

FACING PAGE: From the rooftop bleachers, Beyond the Ivy gets a great view of Wrigley Field.
Photograph by Tony Soluri Photography

is the perfect backdrop for tie-less affairs. Of these rooftops, 1010 Waveland is the most striking and the largest in terms of height and width, featuring lavish amenities including indoor and outdoor food and bar services, as well as bathrooms. Ivan Kutleša knew the structure would be immense and needed to maintain the same slope as the stadium seats. Piece by piece he constructed this extension of Wrigley, designing a steel superstructure, from which the sense atop the bleachers is that one is actually in the stadium, though technically Beyond The Ivy is across the street.

The pride here is the uniqueness of the venue that lends to its versatility to entertain formally and informally. Though covered in ivy, like the field, the chairs are individual, rather than connected, which allows for a friendly amount of hobnobbing. With convenient, elevated barstool trays that are continuous, fans can slide across aisles to catch the game from every angle. There are two grand bars, plasma screen televisions, and fans can enjoy the beer garden too. A group of 200 can reserve Beyond the Ivy for fast-paced events. Fans should not feel they are missing the best of baseball's grub: Some of the tastier menu items include Chicago-style hotdogs, burgers and cookie trays and, the staple beverage of baseball champions, beer.

Located amid four major streets, Wrigley Field has been part of a great, old ballpark tradition, one of the few fields to sit in the heart of the city's downtown area. Fathers and sons still play catch in the street, waiting for homerun balls to fall. Thanks to projects like Beyond the Ivy, the streetscape life of Chicago's home team is able to continue up into the roofs. For Ivan, the great treat is to watch the stadium of his childhood develop into an artistic aesthetic of which he was a part. What more could a fan want? Eamus Catuli! ■ ■ ■ ■ ■ ■ ■ ■ ■ ■ ■

TOP RIGHT: Situated atop the residences of an old, three-story brownstone, this premiere setting is a window to America's favorite pastime.
Photograph by Tony Soluri Photography

BOTTOM RIGHT: Just across Waveland Avenue and left of center field, the atmosphere of the "Friendly Confines" extends Beyond The Ivy.
Photograph by Tony Soluri Photography

FACING PAGE: By far, Beyond the Ivy is the largest rooftop venue to take in a night game since 1988, when the old ballpark was illuminated for evening ballgames.
Photograph by Tony Soluri Photography

The Blackstone Hotel

■ ■

Lucien Lagrange Architects

■ ■ ■ ■ ■ ■ ■ ■ ■ Big decisions need an appropriate setting. Political tides, for example, should not turn at the supermarket. Something classic is needed, something dark—a smoke-filled room. In 1920 Warren G. Harding won the Republican nomination for president, and, although the convention was elsewhere, the nominating committee needed an appropriate setting to find consensus. They met at The Blackstone Hotel—in what one Associated Press reporter would dub "a smoke-filled room." That phrase would stick in the parlance for political decision-making, and The Blackstone Hotel would stick in the political realm as the "Hotel of Presidents," as the building would play a heavy hand in 20th-century politics.

FACING PAGE: The original chandeliers and sconces radiate light throughout the chrysanthemum-carpeted Crystal Ballroom, which has been entrirely restored.
Project Design Team: Lucien Lagrange, Tim Hill, Wayne Miller, Cayl Hollis and Dan Csoka.
Photograph by William Zbaren

Over the last century, and through numerous owners—including Maharishi—The Blackstone Hotel had fallen into disrepair. After closing for a few years during a selling campaign at the turn of the 21st century, the damage became extensive. Eventually, Sage Hospitality Resources bought the property and approached Lucien Lagrange Architects for the redevelopment. Lucien jumped at the rare chance to work on a Classical Revival Beaux-Arts landmark Chicago building. The restoration would involve a total reworking of the interiors, with preservations reserved for historic spaces including the Crystal Ballroom and the original "smoke-filled room."

Lucien asked several key questions. How many rooms would fill the new hotel? What kind of public spaces would exist? Inside, the team managed 332 rooms, with 12 suites, over the 22 stories. With more than 13,000 square feet of meeting spaces, The Blackstone Hotel now features a health spa, a business center and a street-level coffee shop. The inside restoration was technically tough; new heating and plumbing had to function behind the historic finishes. Many of the original chandeliers were even repurchased on eBay. On the exterior, heavy restorations began at the roof. Replicating the color of the original green roof tiles, a new green metal roof maintains a Parisian feel. The façades shoot up in a pillar of red brick and terracotta in a careful, ornate reinstallation.

TOP LEFT: The brick and terracotta exterior defines The Blackstone Hotel and was carefully restored to maintain its look.
Photograph by William Zbaren

TOP RIGHT: Hubbard Place, the "hotel within a hotel," occupies the top three floors of The Blackstone. Within the mansard roof, on the 23rd floor, is an intimate lounge reserved for guests of Hubbard Place, two private boardrooms and four luxury suites.
Photograph by William Zbaren

BOTTOM LEFT: The English Room required the restoration of the original wood paneling and stained glass windows.
Photograph by William Zbaren

FACING PAGE: Walnut paneling and a highly detailed plaster ceiling turn the hotel lobby into a landmark.
Photograph by William Zbaren

There is always a challenge when handling history. People have great stories from The Blackstone Hotel, and therefore the building required careful work under the watchful eyes of the city. Since the hotel is really a part of the Chicago narrative, it was essential for the project not to be a throwback to an old Chicago structure but rather to truly be the structure itself—to maintain the integrity of the building's history and its neighborhood. And for this, Lucien Lagrange Architects has rebuilt a hotel that works well and that is an integral part of the Chicago record. ■ ■ ■ ■ ■ ■ ■ ■ ■ ■

Garmin International Flagship Store

■ ■

Valerio Dewalt Train Associates

■ ■ ■ ■ ■ ■ ■ ■ ■ ■ Here is a game. What image is conjured with "agile"? Perhaps a loosely knotted nautical rope. What about "hip"? Maybe a pair of young Italians sharing a Vespa. "Organic"? Maybe smooth, moss-covered stones. While many words invoke very specific images, such as bagel, the abstract, subjective design game is about hitting the nerves, gut reaction. For Joe Valerio of Valerio Dewalt Train Associates, architectural spaces have high potential for beguiling suggestion.

Offering such architectural mesmerism is Garmin International Flagship Store on Chicago's Magnificent Mile. Garmin designs consumer GPS systems—personal and automotive navigation devices—and for the flagship retail shop, they chose Michigan Avenue for its glamour and great pedestrian traffic and chose Valerio Dewalt Train Associates for its moxie. A company founded and run by engineers, Garmin had never developed its own retail space;

FACING PAGE: Super clear, low-iron glass windows invite passersby into the Garmin flagship store on Chicago's Magnificent Mile.
Project Design Team: Randy Mattheis, Brad Pausha, Anthony Viola, Blake Patten, Maureen Moran and Joe Valerio.
Photograph by Steve Hall, Hedrich Blessing Photography

so the first challenge was to come up with a design concept that captured and communicated the Garmin brand. Garmin needed a people place, needed an image that would attract the public for its first shop, and while engineers and aesthetics often have a prickly relationship, Joe and his team found their clients remarkably adventurous in design.

The deadline was tight. Commissioned in April of 2006, Joe and his team had to finish for a November opening. The aforementioned branding soon began. The building needed to suggest intuition, enablement, accessibility, as well as something dynamic and poetic; the company wanted agile, hip and organic. This building should be equal parts clean, technical and warm. And so Joe went to work. For two months the team held weekly meetings with the clients to reach a design consensus.

The walls became sculptural—a modern aesthetic that embraces passersby. Joe designed these wooden waves on computers, and millworkers bent layers of plywood—ribs, like the hull of a ship—over large sections of what amounted to oversized egg crates. The result is an aesthetic that invites people to literally

TOP LEFT: While the undulating walls suggest the mysteries of the world, Garmin's GPS devices are displayed on custom casework: The power of technology navigates the world's ambiguities.
Photograph by Steve Hall, Hedrich Blessing Photography

BOTTOM LEFT: The second floor of the Garmin store showcases Garmin's aviation and outdoor-related products.
Photograph by Steve Hall, Hedrich Blessing Photography

FACING PAGE LEFT: The signature wood walls are made of Afromosia veneers bent over ribbed frames. The two-story walls unify both levels of the 15,000-square-foot store.
Photograph by Steve Hall, Hedrich Blessing Photography

FACING PAGE RIGHT: The cantilevered staircase presented a challenge to the engineers, the international design consultancy Arup. The stairs carry forward the contrast between the precise and the ambiguous.
Photograph by Steve Hall, Hedrich Blessing Photography

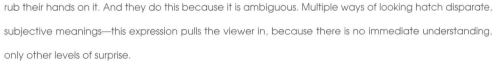

rub their hands on it. And they do this because it is ambiguous. Multiple ways of looking hatch disparate, subjective meanings—this expression pulls the viewer in, because there is no immediate understanding, only other levels of surprise.

In contrast to the sensual wooden walls, the Garmin devices are arrayed on precisely machined custom displays. The displays represent the technical achievement of the products that are used to navigate the mysterious world.

Creating compelling and imaginative spaces like Garmin Flagship Store is the essence of a Valerio Dewalt Train design. These GPS systems are relatively tiny devices—small enough to fit in the palm of your hand. To contain them Garmin needed a big idea, and Joe's sculptural wall was it. Could these walls represent the hull of a ship, a canyon, waves or fenders? The world is full of mystery, and these devices make this puzzling planet comprehensible. Go ahead and touch the walls; perplexity is the beginning of knowledge. ■ ■ ■ ■ ■ ■ ■ ■ ■ ■

Luxbar

■ ■

Shapiro Associates

■ ■ ■ ■ ■ ■ ■ ■ ■ ■ Ever since man invented the stool, he has found comfort bellying up to a bar, ordering the usual from his favorite mixologist, and speaking easy with whomever will listen. In 1908 the innovative architect Adolf Loos designed a pub in Austria called the American Bar. The bar was simple, welcoming and profound—elegant in its reassurance of setting. An austere outer surface hid the classic spirit of comfort and luxury beneath. The owner of a prime spot in the Gold Coast region wanted what Loos delivered—a brilliant twist on the tavern tradition—for an upscale bar of his own. Shapiro Associates, in association with Mark Knauer, responded to the challenge with a cocktail of old saloon conventions and modern aesthetics and created Luxbar.

FACING PAGE: The annex to the main dining room and bar provides a more intimate setting for conversations over dinner.
Project Design Team: Mark Knauer, Beatriz Lopez and Donald Shapiro.
Photograph by Ballogg Photography

Luxbar practically glows at night. The premier European café setting is in a perfect location to see all of the action of the famed Rush Street bar scene from the seats. Part of the design was to bring the seating orientation to the front so that the street life commingled with the bar, in a grand gesture of hospitality. More than a locale that aims simply to provide liquor for the enjoyment of the masses, Luxbar is a study in ambience by a successful restaurateur and a skilled architect.

The materials alone—as a throwback to Loos' design—suggest luxury. The granite and glass exterior breathes a stately air; the interior's elegance pushes for the extra mile: The architect scoured an Italian quarry to find a very specific stone for the front façade, and the rich hand-laid mahogany was installed with Old World workmanship. While these strong materials radiate turn-of-the-century classiness, finding perfection in Luxbar's modernism was a little more difficult. The site is tight, and so, in order to have a full-service kitchen, some subterranean manipulation was required. Beneath the first floor the commercial kitchen stretches all the way to the street, which allows heating units to warm the street-level patio for those colder Chicago nights. The second floor, meanwhile, functions not only as overflow for Luxbar's popular weekend nights but also as a great banquet space.

Shapiro Associates spent a year on the design—with interior design by Mark Knauer—and two years on the construction of Luxbar. Always with an eye toward perpetuating the bar's great ambience, Donald Shapiro finds himself popping back in, maybe installing new fixtures or refurbishing some of the elements, so that as Chicagoans progress through the years, Luxbar will, too. The new staple of Gold Coast taverns, Luxbar is Shapiro Associates at its finest. ■ ■ ■ ■ ■ ■ ■

RIGHT: The transparency of the street façade draws street traffic to the bar. The stone was fabricated and book-matched by craftsmen in Italy.
Photograph by Ballogg Photography

FACING PAGE TOP: Mirrors surround the stair to the second-floor bar to expand the experience.
Photograph by Ballogg Photography

FACING PAGE BOTTOM: The main-floor bar details and materials reflect on time past.
Photograph by Ballogg Photography

Makray Memorial Golf Clubhouse

■ ■

Gillespie Design Group

■ ■ ■ ■ ■ ■ ■ ■ ■ ■ Barrington is an exclusive community that sits 40 minutes northwest of Chicago. Paul Makray purchased Thunderbird Golf Course in

Barrington in 1962 and improved it each year. However, when Paul passed away in 1999, his family made the decision to completely redesign and rebuild

the golf course—literally moving hills, providing several new water features and an all new course layout—changing the name to Makray Memorial Golf

Club, in honor of Paul. The Makray family desired that the clubhouse, too, be on par with the newly refurbished course, and Gillespie Design Group came

in for the task.

The Makrays, of course, were looking for something upscale for the new clubhouse to fit within the context of the community. Gillespie Design Group

originally designed a two-level clubhouse that had a French Country flair—a fashionable style in this vicinity. But a funny thing happened. The owner took

FACING PAGE: The Scottish influence is apparent at Makray Memorial Golf Clubhouse in Barrington.
Photograph by Interesting Developments, Inc.

a trip to Scotland right in the midst of the course's refurbishment. He was clearly impressed with the birthplace of golf and came back with a new idea. The golf course should be extended to 7,000 yards and the clubhouse should look more Scottish.

So Gillespie Design Group designed the clubhouse . . . again. They did a good deal of research to find out everything they could about Scottish castles, manors and clubhouses. They looked to the windswept coast of the North Sea and the legendary golf clubs of Scotland for inspiration. The new clubhouse picks up on the massive stone and stucco structures with punched-opening windows, large chimney features and steep, sloped roofs, reminiscent of older Scottish structures. Even the wood is distressed to maintain the authentic look. Because of the expanded length of the golf course, the building footprint is smaller than the original design. Now at three levels, the pro-shop and grille are on the main level and the locker rooms and cart storage are on the lower. The banquet area is lifted to the upper level with a grand balcony to take advantage of the tremendous views down the 10th and 18th fairways.

LEFT: From the grand balcony the terrace is seen below.
Photograph by Interesting Developments, Inc.

FACING PAGE TOP: The back of the clubhouse overlooks the 10th and 18th fairways.
Photograph by Interesting Developments, Inc.

FACING PAGE BOTTOM: Stone, stucco and slate were used for the building's façade.
Photograph by Interesting Developments, Inc.

David Gillespie and his team met frequently with the Makray group throughout the design and building process. Open communication and a good collaborative relationship with the owner is the best route to a winning project. Gillespie Design Group is a talented, experienced team with an extensive portfolio of successful projects throughout the Midwest. And their Makray Memorial Golf Clubhouse not only commemorates the father of a noble family, but also is the crowning centerpiece of one of the Chicago area's finest courses. ■ ■ ■ ■ ■ ■ ■ ■ ■

Meadows Club

■ ■

Arzoumanian & Company

■ ■ ■ ■ ■ ■ ■ ■ ■ ■ Well known in the Indian community of Chicago as a visionary businessman, Madan Kulkarni, the owner of the new Meadows Club in Rolling Meadows, Illinois, had a dream of creating a social and cultural oasis in the vast retail and technology landscape of Chicago's burgeoning northwest suburbs. Far beyond simply catering to business meetings and special events, he envisioned customized facilities for art, music, dance and gastronomy—as well as state of the art space for social functions, meetings and conventions—all under one very large roof. Following the first-phase construction of a 16,000-square-foot banquet/meeting hall, Meadows Club plans to add a 1,000-seat performing arts theater, an international-cuisine restaurant, jazz bar, art gallery, art academy and two recording studios. While still evolving, the first phase of the project has been lauded as a resounding success.

Facing Page: Meadows Club's expansive glass front reflects the constant motion of the superhighway at its doorstep, creating a dynamic façade symbolizing the ever-changing activity within.
Photograph by Patsy McEnroe

These grand dreams came with unusual challenges for the project architect. The space chosen to realize Kulkarni's vision was "literally a shed which had been an indoor tennis club barely protected from the elements," said Raffi Arzoumanian, AIA, NCARB. At the most conceptual level, Raffi and team leader Joanna Zywczyk, Associate AIA, were faced with the task of creating an accessible space for 1,000 people to get in and out when the only access was on one side of the building. The team created a "highway" on one side of the building that facilitates traffic flow and allows guests, who likely have never been inside the building before, to get oriented within the large space very quickly.

Among the other challenges of repurposing the structure was accommodating opposing space and functional needs that could potentially occur simultaneously in proximity to one another. The design specifications had to allow for the possibility of disco music in the banquet hall at the same time as a classical music concert in the auditorium next door, and the installation of a recording studio within earshot of the jazz bar. Arzoumanian & Company took advantage of the vast spans within the existing interior supporting structure to house the large spaces.

TOP LEFT: Even when set to capacity, the main banquet hall exudes warmth and grace with discreet touches of Old World ornamentation.
Photograph by Patsy McEnroe

BOTTOM LEFT: The soaring pre-function lobby is easily adaptable to a variety of uses.
Photograph by Patsy McEnroe

FACING PAGE: Richly stained and detailed woodworking sets a dignified backdrop for the elegant furnishings of the main banquet hall.
Photograph by Patsy McEnroe

Special-use spaces were located in a new addition and buffered with sound barriers. Adept at acquiring technical knowledge to address concerns like sound transmission, Arzoumanian & Company provided the client with levels of expertise usually reserved for specialists in the field, and collaborated closely with the principal interior designer, Swapna Sathyan, on material specifications that supported the owner's vision for grand and inviting interior spaces.

To give a distinctive identity to the highly visible structure, which is located between the I-90 superhighway and a prominent brick office complex directly to the east, Arzoumanian & Company set off the exterior of Meadows Club visually with contrasting colors and large panes of glass to create immediate prominence for a most unusual new structure. ■ ■ ■ ■ ■ ■ ■ ■ ■ ■

Navy Pier

VOA Associates, Incorporated
BTA Benjamin Thompson & Associates

In 1911 Charles Sumner Frost was elected by the Harbor and Sewer Commission of the City of Chicago to design a municipal pier into Lake Michigan. Construction of the 3,000-foot-long, 292-foot-wide pier was begun in 1914. By the summer of 1916, the pier was open to the public, complete with a Head House, freight and passenger buildings, a terminal building and the recreational East End Ballroom with its 100-foot-high, half-dome ceiling. The pier quickly became a destination point for the citizens of Chicago. Since its revitalization in the mid-1990s, this mixed-use convention and entertainment facility has become the number one tourist attraction in the state of Illinois and returns a valuable public recreation and exposition institution to the citizens of Chicago.

ABOVE: Navy Pier is an integral part of the Chicago lakefront, as well as a premier tourist destination.
Photograph by Vito Palmisano

FACING PAGE: The tensile structure of the Skyline Stage and the brightly lit Ferris wheel on Navy Pier are recognizable landmarks on the Chicago skyline.
Photograph by Vito Palmisano

VOA Associates, Incorporated and BTA won a national design competition to transform Navy Pier into a vital, creative public amenity, connected to the city's lakefront park system, which would be economically viable as a convention facility, as well as a public destination. The redesign included creating an entirely new infrastructure. Vehicular traffic would be to the north and pedestrian traffic along the south dock. The original Head House and the structures to the east of the Terminal Building would remain and be restored, while the intervening freight sheds would be demolished to make way for the new convention and entertainment facilities. The pier was widened by 50 feet to the north to provide additional space for the anticipated service and public vehicular traffic, as well as a waterfront pedestrian promenade.

Amenities on Navy Pier are varied and plentiful. IMAX 3D was inaugurated at the Navy Pier IMAX Theater in March 1996. Navy Pier's IMAX Theater, seating 440, presents large format IMAX films on a 5,500-square-foot screen over six stories in height.

The State of Illinois Board of Tourism and the City of Chicago Department of Cultural Affairs combined to establish the 3,700-square-foot Illinois Market Place. This unique store provides tourist information and retail merchandising within a bevy of designs.

"Skyline Stage" at Navy Pier, completed in May 1994, is a flexible, seasonal outdoor venue that takes advantage of Chicago's beautiful skyline and summer climate. Truly an outdoor "theater" with a complete stagehouse, rigging sets, multiuse sound system, flexible acoustics, orchestra shell, technical balconies, control rooms and orchestra pit, this tensile structure is a public home for Chicago's diverse performing arts interests.

With more than 170,000 square feet of exhibition space and 48,000 square feet of meeting rooms, Festival Hall connects to the existing historic buildings on the east end and is one of Chicago's most popular and versatile destinations for special events, exhibits and meetings. The 19,000-square-foot Grand Ballroom is one of Chicago's best-known public spaces, where debutantes, businessmen, politicians and socialites have been awed by its magnificent domed ceiling and spectacular lakeside scenery.

The Chicago Shakespeare Theater is an additional phase to Navy Pier that consists of an intimate 530-seat theater to host a range of performances and a flexible 200-seat studio theater above the main stage for smaller shows. The design enables the theater to accommodate various stage and scenery configurations and provides state-of-the-art sound, lighting and technical-support facilities. In addition, the theater includes a rehearsal hall, an English pub, a bookstore, support spaces and facilities for educational workshops, seminars and outreach programs.

The main family attraction is the new Family Pavilion, which incorporates the historic Head House, the pier's westernmost building. Rides, games, retail kiosks, restaurants and a food court provide a wealth of opportunities for family fun. ■ ■ ■ ■ ■ ■ ■ ■ ■ ■

Ping Tom Memorial Park

Site Design Group, Ltd.

■ ■ ■ ■ ■ ■ ■ ■ ■ With the opening of the Dan Ryan Freeway in the 1960s, Chinatown lost its only park land, and for the next 40 years the people of Chinatown waited for a new outdoor space. The lead proponent for the new green space was Ping Tom, a Chinese American businessman renowned for his civic leadership. Though he passed away in 1995, his vision came to fruition in 1999 as Ping Tom Memorial Park. When finally the movement came to build the park, Site Design Group, headed by Ernest C. Wong, jumped at the opportunity to develop the new pride and joy of Chinatown.

The site's feng shui, however, contained many elements of concern for the community. Six acres in size, the site was formerly an old railyard, butting against the Chicago River. A very linear property, the space faces a chaotic onslaught of transportation modes. With boats on the river, the 18th Street

ABOVE: Ornamental grasses line the pathways of Ping Tom Memorial Park, leading visitors through a gentle flowing series of spaces.
Photograph by Ron Gordon

FACING PAGE: The four-dragon gateway greets visitors to Ping Tom Memorial Park.
Project Design Team: Ernest C. Wong, Robert K. Sit and Frances Maravelea.
Photograph by Ron Gordon

Bridge, Amtrak and other public transports, the urban setting created complex challenges. Site Design Group cleverly programmed the park so that once inside, the white noise disappears and a quiet stillness triumphs amidst the industrial world.

The team wanted the park to communicate the vibrant community in a cultural way, something that serves identity as well as destination. Carefully researching the classical Chinese gardens of Suzhou, Ernie Wong learned how these gardens were constructed as spaces within spaces, with framed views. He used this classical method in a modern sense. Once past the railroads, visitors walk through four dragon columns that symbolize the first courtyard. The columns face north—to the power of the city—and have an inset paving that calls for "happiness." One literally has to walk around the center—through garden pieces—to gain access to the river and the classically styled pavilion, the meandering experience of discovery.

Through careful manipulation of earthforms, Site Design Group turned the face of the park toward the river. Initially, the space focused toward the railroad tracks—a less than pleasant point of view. By dropping the river edge of the park 15 feet, the firm created a terrace to the river—similar to the rice patties in Asia—drawing the eye to the water. As time progresses, Ping Tom Memorial Park's additional phases will push for connections, searching for communal identity in public spaces, by enhancing the dichotomy of urban space and tranquility. As both kite-flying and large civic events permeate the park, Ping Tom Memorial Park was also the final destination for a season of *The Amazing Race.* Clearly, Chinatown has found its new heart. ■ ■ ■ ■ ■ ■ ■ ■ ■ ■

ABOVE: Ping Tom continues to inspire Chicago's Chinatown community.
Photograph by Robert Sit

FACING PAGE TOP: Chicago's skyline frames the urban oasis of this river park.
Photograph by Ernest C. Wong

FACING PAGE BOTTOM: The children's playground serves as a focal point for this linear park.
Photograph by Ron Gordon

Soldier Field and North Burnham Park Redevelopment

■ ■

Wood + Zapata
Lohan Caprile Goettsch Architects

■ ■ ■ ■ ■ ■ ■ ■ ■ ■ Chicago is known as a bold city. Nothing speaks this louder than its architecture. When the Chicago Bears and the Chicago Park District decided it was time to bring Soldier Field into the new millennium, they wanted a bold building, one that would both reach to the future and recall the past; Soldier Field is named to honor the soldiers of World War I, and so the new stadium is a study of the dichotomy of old and new. The project was a joint venture of two architecture firms: Wood + Zapata (now Ben Wood Studio Shanghai and Carlos Zapata Studio) and Lohan Caprile Goettsch Architects (now Goettsch Partners). Wood + Zapata was primarily responsible for the architectural design of the Soldier Field stadium, and Lohan Caprile Goettsch Architects was primarily responsible for the master plan and North Burnham Park project.

FACING PAGE: The modern stadium fits within the tight confines of the historic structure while establishing a clear contrast between old and new.
Project Design Team: Benjamin Wood, Carlos Zapata, Dirk Lohan, Joseph Caprile, Anthony Montalto, Joseph Dolinar and Basil W.C. Souder.
Photograph by David B. Seide, © Defined Space

The Bears had been shortchanged with clubs, concessions and skyboxes in the original stadium. While bringing in all of the expected modern conveniences to the new facility, the design team took an innovative approach, challenging all of the typical assumptions in stadium design. Because of the narrowness of the site, a standard NFL stadium bowl would not fit. So, the architects created one of the most unique seating decks in the country. By reconfiguring pieces of the decks, Soldier Field has an architectural exchange, as the state-of-the-art suites cantilever over the stadium seats. This elongated massing overlaps, sloping toward the field in points and offering some of the closest seats to the action in pro football.

The four-level suites feature high-tech, anti-reflective glass walls and innovative mechanical systems. One may notice that grass starts growing earlier at the new Soldier Field and that it continues to grow long into the season. This is due to subterranean heating—hot water piped underneath and across the field. The original stadium was surrounded by paved parking lots. Today, the stadium sits within 17 acres of new parkland and accommodates additional parking in a new underground garage. Meanwhile, North Burnham Park is now a united museum campus, bringing together the Field Museum, Shedd Aquarium and Adler Planetarium, in addition to the stadium and new public amenities.

The Chicago Bears and the Chicago Park District have taken extra steps in turning the lakeside site into one of the most impressive destinations in town. In fact, Soldier Field is the only stadium to have its own snow-making machine for the sledding hill just outside. This, in the end, is one of those rare projects that embodies the spirit of the city. ■ ■ ■ ■ ■ ■ ■ ■ ■ ■

ABOVE: The formerly antiquated stadium, surrounded by acres of paved parking, has been transformed into a vibrant sports-and-entertainment facility set within a park along Chicago's lakefront.
Photograph by David B. Seide, © Defined Space

FACING PAGE TOP: The historic colonnades are juxtaposed against the sweeping, contemporary steel-and-glass stadium.
Photograph by Doug Fogelson/DRFP

FACING PAGE BOTTOM: The north end of the stadium highlights the structure's asymmetrical configuration, along with an entry promenade and water wall, dedicated to all branches of military service.
Photograph by David B. Seide, © Defined Space

Superdawg

■ ■

Shapiro Associates

■ ■ ■ ■ ■ ■ ■ ■ ■ ■ Since 1948, from the top of a building in Chicago's Norwood Park neighborhood, delightfully anthropomorphic Maurie and Flaurie have been beckoning passersby into Superdawg, one of the few original drive-in restaurants left. Superdawg has a long history of heralding the superiority of the Chicago-style hot dog: a weird and wonderful concoction of spicy frankfurter, relish, mustard, onion, pickle spear, pickled green tomato wedge, peppers and a poppy-seed bun.

Architect Donald Shapiro, AIA, knew the owners of Superdawg were looking for a little change. The original Superdawg building was a very distinct, 20-by-12-foot box that for years served its function. But the owners spent 25 years considering a new building, and in 1999, engaged Shapiro Associates for the exciting renovation. The plan was to expand and remodel this mid-century, retro structure without losing any of its endearing characteristics, and without closing.

FACING PAGE: The saw-tooth edge of the canopies is reflective of the blue and white diamonds that decorate everything from the floors to the napkins.
Project Design Team: Kenneth Lee and Donald Shapiro.
Photograph by Ballogg Photography

To proceed, Shapiro Associates often worked through the night, building around the old structure. They paved the gravel lot, installed neon-studded canopies for weather protection, and added a new dining area to the walk-up and drive-in options. By expressing the original look, Shapiro Associates developed what could only be described as a total funk edifice: a great bit of Americana and a throwback to that lost era of retro-futurism, where control towers and blinking lights make liftoff seem inevitable.

Assimilating Chicago iconography into the present and beyond can be a bit of a pickle, but Donald certainly relished the opportunity. His long-term relationship with the proprietors of Superdawg is not just the transformation of a family's lifelong propulsion of that most American of foods—the hot dog—but the project itself is a statement in the sustaining power of originality. And as long as those two 12-foot icons blink atop Superdawg, people will find themselves driving in to experience good food and incredible architecture, two of Chicago's favorite pastimes. ■ ■ ■ ■ ■ ■ ■ ■ ■ ■ ■

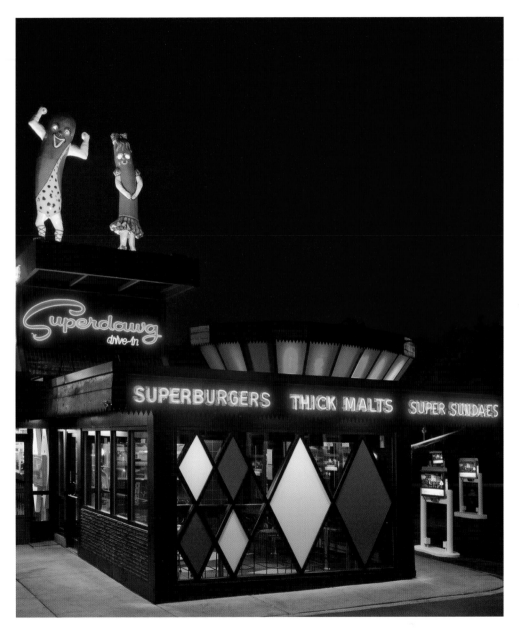

ABOVE: The new dining room looks like part of the original structure and provides an alternative to eating inside your car.
Photograph by Ballogg Photography

RIGHT: Maurie and Flaurie made a brief trip to Wisconsin for refurbishing while the wooden sign structure was replaced with steel.
Photograph by Ballogg Photography

FACING PAGE TOP: The "carhop-in-a-wire" electronic speaker system predates drive-thru technology.
Photograph by Ballogg Photography

FACING PAGE BOTTOM: The new canopies needed to appear like they were always there.
Photograph by Ballogg Photography

Woodlands at the Promenade

■ ■

Techcon Dallas, Inc.

■ ■ ■ ■ ■ ■ ■ ■ ■ For years legions of Frank Lloyd Wright aficionados have trekked from near and far to the Chicago suburb of Oak Park to experience firsthand the legend's remarkable design prowess, which has long been on display via many of the village's extraordinary residences. Just outside of Chicago in Bolingbrook, the Woodlands at the Promenade has afforded discerning patrons the opportunity to dine on innovative American cuisine and relax in an engaging restaurant setting that pays homage to America's most well-known architect. Designed by Bruce Russo of Techcon Dallas, the Woodlands at the Promenade is a must-visit dining experience for even the most casual of architecture followers—a place where the interior ambience and architectural nuances rival the contemporary American menu offerings for top billing and draw visitors back again and again.

FACING PAGE: Welcomed by warm hues and various textures, cascading water stimulates the senses as you enter—nourishment for every sense.
Project Design Team: Bruce Russo, Joe Russo, Laura Fate and Victor Badillo.
Photograph by Scott Hagar

The Woodlands at the Promenade was inspired primarily by Fallingwater—voted the "best all-time work of American architecture" in 1991 by AIA members—yet collectively represents a sophisticated amalgam of many Wrightian designs: elements from the Prairie Style vernacular he perfected in Oak Park, his design studio, Oak Park's Unity Temple and other extraordinary creations. However, the renowned Fallingwater was at the forefront, guiding the design to its remarkable built-out composition, and is evidenced in specific design elements throughout.

Located at the Promenade Bolingbrook, the Woodlands' architecture is defined by its natural stone, exquisite hardwoods and clean, contemporary lines—all of which are deftly assembled within a strong horizontal motif, a prominent thread running through the vast majority of Wright's work. Arrival at the restaurant is denoted by passage through a front entrance flanked by waterfalls on either side, while the bar is elevated with a water feature underneath to simulate the creek at Fallingwater. The interior is awash with natural stones and woods that create a wholly engaging interior aura, which is at once relaxing and inviting. Moreover, the ceiling topography varies throughout the restaurant, creating intimate niches throughout the space and a sense of comfortable sophistication.

An engaging contemporary architectural solution paying homage to a local legend, the Woodlands at the Promenade is the perfect backdrop for leisure and forward-thinking American fare, such as cedar plank citrus salmon and mahogany chicken, to name a few. Designed by Techcon Dallas, this unique restaurant offering has brought a new local flavor to metropolitan Chicago, and has enjoyed such great success that it has spawned additional locations throughout the United States in such locales as Dallas and Colorado. ■ ■ ■ ■

TOP RIGHT: The sound of trickling water envelops the entire restaurant as the river rock laden water feature wraps around the bar.
Photograph by Scott Hagar

BOTTOM RIGHT: The main dining room showcases elaborate high ceilings and an oversized fireplace that grounds the room as its main focal point.
Photograph by Scott Hagar

FACING PAGE TOP: The south dining room is handsomely appointed with stacked stone and simple furnishings reminiscent of Wright's sense of style.
Photograph by Scott Hagar

FACING PAGE BOTTOM: Clean lines and stone adornments add grandeur accented by strategic lighting, showcasing architecture evocative of Wright's period.
Photograph by Scott Hagar

CHAPTER TWO
Urban Living

Urban living has been revitalized in many cities that had once lost much of their vitality to urban sprawl, resulting in a recharged ambience, buildings bustling about with activity and convenient access to downtown living and working. These pages represent the finest examples of how an architectural vision can transform and improve the landscape and quality of life for city dwellers.

Whether it is a mixed-use building that combines residential units and retail space or a multifamily residence cropping up in place of abandoned buildings or land, the firms involved in these substantial projects undertake not only the logistics of planning, creating and executing the design, they realize the impact their project will have on the growth and success of their native city. Chicago residences like Lucien Lagrange Architects' Park Tower and Mesa Developments' The Heritage and The Legacy are sure to impress.

The architects' diverse attitudes and thoughts behind their buildings may fascinate or even surprise. One aspect that weaves a common thread throughout these projects is the commitment to elevating the quality of life for many. Yet these projects also offer the opportunity to make their mark on their city's history. After all, the multifamily and mixed-use spaces will serve as homes and places of business for generations to follow.

River Village Pointe, Hirsch Associates LLC, page 118

Optima Old Orchard Woods, David Hovey, FAIA Architect, Optima, Inc., page 70

Erie on the Park, Lucien Lagrange Architects, page 98

Optima Old Orchard Woods

■ ■

David Hovey, FAIA Architect, Optima, Inc.

■ ■ ■ ■ ■ ■ ■ ■ ■ ■ When David Hovey sets his eyes on a space, one can be sure that, soon enough, something miraculous will blossom. For 10 years, he pined for the woods; 20 miles north of downtown Chicago, at the skirt of the Harms Woods Forest Preserve, sat an extraordinary location, for which he envisioned a grand-scale architectural venture, what would become the awe-inspiring Optima Old Orchard Woods condominiums. This massive residential community is so ensconced in forestry, so aware of the surrounding environment and the land on which it sits, chills would run up the spine of any transcendentalist.

FACING PAGE: Three towers interconnect with bridge-like residences and extended terraces to create a dynamic, sculptural place next to the serene setting of the protected forest preserve to the west.
Project Design Team: Tod Desmarais, Matt Cison, Roman Wachula, Mike Schwerzler and Bill Duke.
Photograph by Jon Miller, Hedrich Blessing Photography

The views alone can stop a heart. Miles of forest stretch to the west—undulating planes of green preserved by Daniel Burnham for Chicago at the early 20th century; to the east, the blue mirror of Lake Michigan, the largest freshwater lake in the United States; to the south, the remarkable Chicago skyline. These views are imperative to achieving a wonderful sense of scale, a sense of place. What is abundantly clear is that maintaining a provincial sense amidst the modernity of Chicago plays a great role in David's project.

Optima Old Orchard Woods has a unique location, for it straddles community and countryside. Major transportation arteries, such as the Edens Expressway, are just moments away, which is perfect for this tall, very large residential structure for sheer convenience, offering a community setting unlike any around. The building itself is not one giant mass, but rather three interlocking towers, each creating multistory openings with unique views. These variegated volumes do two things: First and functionally, they allowed Optima to build systematically in sections, opening one tower before the crew moved to the next; second and aesthetically, the play with positive and negative spaces breaks uniformity, ensuring that from any angle Optima Old Orchard Woods is an elegant, highly sculptural complex with ever-changing views.

LEFT: The inner courtyard is elegantly landscaped and leads to the entry of each tower. The parking structure is smartly integrated for convenience, yet is barely perceptible from the courtyard.
Photograph by Jon Miller, Hedrich Blessing Photography

FACING PAGE LEFT: The brick-paved entry drive is framed by columns of an elevated promenade. The massive fountain with playful jets of water creates a soothing focal point for the courtyard.
Photograph by Bill Timmerman

FACING PAGE RIGHT: The two-story, sunlit lobbies of each tower are luxuriously appointed with materials of white marble and terrazzo.
Photograph by Bill Timmerman

The lawn stretches out with lush, English-style gardens, while a series of fountains suggest a very paternal space, all somewhat reminiscent of, perhaps, downtown 19th-century London, but with more height. As the pond reflects both the gardens and the forest preserve, a relation to the building becomes apparent, for the continuing of planes gives a bold, positive identity to this landscaped quadrangle, rather than something timid.

All of Optima Old Orchard Woods' roofs are green. It was David's intent to extend the ideas of the forest and apply preservation to his building. Along with landscaped roofs—one in particular is a quarter of an acre of verdant greens—Old Orchard Woods uses high volumes of natural light, made possible by floor-to-ceiling glass. Natural materials also contribute to the building's environmental concerns: granite counters, wooden cabinets, wood or stone floors, all provided to exude warmth and to be ecologically friendly.

ABOVE LEFT: Sun-drenched rooms are common throughout the complex, which features floor-to-ceiling glass in all residences.
Photograph by Bill Timmerman

ABOVE RIGHT: Master bathrooms are appointed with lavish finishes, such as travertine tile, cabinets of figured maple and countertops of marble.
Photograph by Bill Timmerman

FACING PAGE: The two-story sunlit pool space seems nestled into the treetops. The quiet combination of water, trees and natural light creates a soothing spa-like space.
Photograph by Bill Timmerman

For David, one of the great opportunities with this project was the chance to provide upscale amenities for the residents. Homeowners may meet with a buyer liaison group, provided by Optima to ensure that units are suited to the individual. The upgrade material offered is of the highest quality. The common spaces at Optima Old Orchard Woods are very functional and quite impressive, including a luxurious party room and a monumental swimming pool. Each tower also has a high-tech, state-of-the-art exercise facility. Inside there is a grocery store, beauty salon and a dry cleaner. And along with various offices, a promenade deck offers great solitary moments in the sun. So rather than being self-contained, Optima Old Orchard Woods is a brilliant example of convenience, understanding both the human call to nature, as well as the communal draw of the city.

Whether viewed from the exterior or interior, close at hand or far in the distance, Optima Old Orchard Woods radiates firmness, commodity and delight. The mix of tenants, from first time buyers to empty-nesters, adds a human vitality to the building, and proves that there is no limit to ideas. The function and beauty of Optima Old Orchard Woods verifies once again that David Hovey is a master builder. ■ ■ ■ ■ ■ ■ ■ ■ ■ ■

TOP RIGHT: Open kitchens are of sumptuous materials such as natural cherry and reflective granite. Top-of-the-line appliances are integrated within cabinetry to create an elegant, finished space.
Photograph by Bill Timmerman

BOTTOM RIGHT: While the west-facing views of the woods change dynamically with the time of day and season, their status is protected as part of the Harms Woods Forest Preserve.
Photograph by Bill Timmerman

FACING PAGE LEFT: Jets of water play in the sun at the promenade that connects the north and south towers. Water sounds create a soothing atmosphere and can be heard from many residences.
Photograph by Bill Timmerman

FACING PAGE RIGHT: Open living spaces of some homes lead to green roof areas where residents can enjoy terraces in the sky.
Photograph by Bill Timmerman

160 East Illinois Street

■ ■

Built Form, LLC

■ ■ ■ ■ ■ ■ ■ ■ ■ Respected for building multifamily residences in and around Chicago, Residential Homes of America saw great potential in 160 East Illinois Street, a premium downtown address. The existing low-rise brick building was under-utilized, and the firm envisioned a potent building form for a new luxury residence with convenient retail space and parking. Built Form was commissioned for the design—a testament to its expansive architectural repertoire—and the product of this collaboration yielded one of the finest multifamily residences in the community.

True to its mantra of creating architecture that balances contemporary sensibilities with lasting significance, Built Form—in collaboration with the architect of record, OWP/P—deftly executed the idea of an urban home that relates to its prominent location just steps from Michigan Avenue and close proximity to the famed Wrigley building. 160 East Illinois is a contemporary response to the Art Deco style of the adjacent InterContinental Chicago hotel and

FACING PAGE: The east elevation of the building faces Lake Michigan.
Project Design Team: Robert Bistry, Arden Freeman, Richard Parks, Stephen Poston and Michan Walker.
Photograph by Alan Shortall

functions as a landmark in its own right. Filling the site in all directions to maximize living space, the volume of the building is shaped to respond to the form of the adjacent hotel. The double entrances—one of which is elevated 18 feet above the other—open graciously to intersecting streets. While the north/south elevations respond to the hotel, the east-facing façade, comprised entirely of glass, maximizes views to the lake.

With an exterior of concrete, aluminum rain-screens and precast concrete panels, the 26-story building blends harmoniously with its surroundings. The 133 luxury residences possess the same contemporary aesthetic as the exterior, which appeals to urban dwellers young and seasoned.

The principals of Built Form have completed a number of urban high-rise residential buildings, yet the striking architectural form of 160 East Illinois, along with its relationship to the site context, make this one of the most notable additions to the firm's portfolio. Acknowledging but not copying the neighboring architecture—and revealing this relationship while relating to the larger context of urban Chicago—160 East Illinois is a sophisticated addition to the urban skyline.

TOP LEFT: Careful massing develops a unique relationship with the existing hotel.
Photograph by Alan Shortall

BOTTOM LEFT: The base of the building hits St. Clair Street, a prime Chicago walking spot.
Photograph by Alan Shortall

FACING PAGE LEFT: A view of the building from Michigan Avenue reveals its rapport with the Tribune Tower and InterContinental hotel.
Photograph by Alan Shortall

FACING PAGE RIGHT: In immediate context, the overall building takes its stand.
Photograph by Alan Shortall

5350 South Shore Drive

■ ■

Nicholas Clark Architects, Ltd.

■ ■ ■ ■ ■ ■ ■ ■ ■ ■ Rare is the opportunity for architects to enhance the fabric of a Chicago neighborhood with a ground-up design that overlooks Lake Michigan. At 5350 South Shore Drive, where a synagogue once stood, the principals of Nicholas Clark Architects created an exquisite enclave of 44 townhome units. The enduring design of limestone and rhythmically placed bay windows and balconies blends harmoniously with the area's established architectural vernacular, yet its modern flair sets it well apart from the standard rowhouse model that has been rampantly reproduced throughout the city. 5350 South Shore Drive endeavors not to replicate older buildings; rather, it takes cues from its historical neighbors—including the proximate University of Chicago—and presents itself as a timeless example of architecture meant for contemporary city living.

FACING PAGE: The private courtyard provides a quiet respite for residents.
Project Design Team: Peter Nicholas, Ann Clark, Lane Fowlie, Edward Heinen and Richard Blender.
Photograph by Linda Oyama Bryan

Designing for an urban area such as the Hyde Park area of Chicago requires sincere ingenuity: The sites are tight, so maximizing interior living and exterior leisure space is of the essence. Within 5350 South Shore Drive, there are a variety of floorplans—1,800- to 3,600-square-foot units and plenty of variation in between—ensuring that the architecture will appeal to a broad spectrum of home seekers and, therefore, be enjoyed well into the future. Unique among such developments, all of 5350 South Shore Drive's units boast exceptional views of Lake Michigan, the city lights or the expansive landscaped courtyard. The units that face the lake are accessed via private stairways that separate the living space from the ground plane,

affording residents security and privacy. Those same units are defined by monumental bay elements with floor-to-ceiling glass that provides natural illumination and unobstructed views of the water.

While it is virtually impossible for every residence within a townhome community to overlook the skyline or water, principals Peter Nicholas and Ann Clark created a courtyard space organized by a meandering path of verdant landscaping and inviting wooden benches. In contrast to the more civic-scaled lakefront façade, the courtyard façades are comprised of a mixture of materials, including red brick, limestone,

aluminum panels and obscured glass privacy screens that provide a human scale. Residents benefit twofold: From inside, they enjoy carefully framed vignettes of the courtyard; while outside, they mingle with neighbors in a natural, peaceful oasis from the fast pace of the city.

Nicholas Clark Architects gleaned inspiration for 5350 South Shore Drive from the site's inherent assets and the historical quality of its surroundings and allowed each element to evolve organically in order to enhance and complement these conditions. Replete with private decks, balconies, discrete garages and even a trio of greenhouses, the townhome community is compatible with the world around it while projecting a stately yet uniquely welcoming personality. ■ ■ ■ ■ ■ ■ ■ ■ ■ ■

ABOVE: Lantern-like glass bays topped by balconies orient toward lake views and punctuate the solid limestone façade wall. Monumental stairs and metal canopies lead to the second-floor unit entries.
Photograph by Linda Oyama Bryan

RIGHT: Limestone on the street-facing elevation lends a monolithic quality and civic scale, while aluminum panels define entry to the courtyard, auto court and individual units.
Photograph by Linda Oyama Bryan

FACING PAGE LEFT: The end units in the courtyard provide a visual terminus and vaulted living and dining room space for the unit owners.
Photograph by Linda Oyama Bryan

FACING PAGE RIGHT: A mix of different cladding materials, balconies, private patios and landscape elements provide a human scale in the courtyard.
Photograph by Linda Oyama Bryan

65 East Goethe

■ ■

Fordham Company

■ ■ ■ ■ ■ ■ ■ ■ ■ ■ In the late 1800s, the Palmer Mansion established the Gold Coast as prime real estate—since then it has been one of the most affluent neighborhoods in the world. Home to some of the wealthiest people in the country, this turn-of-the-century neighborhood sits low and looks out over the lake. In a district with such high-end profiling, residences become a challenge for any developer. However, Fordham Company is well-versed in the development of elegant, residential structures; its 65 East Goethe is a French Beaux-Arts jewel box in a neighborhood of timeless classics.

Because of its historical setting, 65 East—as it has come to be known—took four-and-a-half years to get zoned for eight residential stories; yet it was clearly worth the effort. Christopher T. Carley, Fordham Company's founder, wanted a Parisian personality for the building, to fit into the classic architecture of buildings going back as far as 1870. He commissioned Lucien Lagrange as his French connection. This fine example of Beaux-Arts was the second largest

FACING PAGE: Styled in the architectural detail of Paris in the 1800s, 65 East Goethe stands stately in the heart of the storied Gold Coast and steps from Lake Michigan beaches. Photograph by William Zbaren

limestone project in the country at the time of construction. The French doors and windows—framed in solid mahogany—and Juliet balconies of hand-forged iron capture the flair of Europe; but it is the mansard roof, clad in zinc and punctuated by portal windows, that fulfills the Parisian identity.

But 65 East is the best of both the Beaux-Arts and modern worlds. A 6,000-square-foot garden sits at the rooftop. This great common space features native flora and unbeatable views of Lake Michigan just steps away. The 18 residences—four of which are maisonettes—range from 3,500 to 12,000 square feet, with up to 12-foot ceilings and all of the modern comforts and security. With lots of stone and glass, and a fair amount of arches, 65 East has incorporated essential elements to pay homage to the old architectural flair for the new world.

65 East Goethe has become home to the who's who of the Chicago elite. As the flagship for a new type of modern elegance, 65 East garners a high price tag. However, with 20 years of exclusively high-end developing, Fordham Company can boast of its oeuvre of well-heeled indulgences. A beautiful and one-of-a-kind addition to Chicago and the Gold Coast, 65 East Goethe is an architectural wonder and the new definition of luxury living. ■ ■ ■ ■ ■ ■ ■ ■ ■ ■

RIGHT: A unique Fordham design provides first-floor masonette residents with their own private entries, with easy access to the main lobby and secure underground parking.
Photograph by William Zbaren

FACING PAGE LEFT: Hand-forged ornamental ironwork creates a dramatic entry for the residents of 65 East.
Photograph by William Zbaren

FACING PAGE RIGHT: Each home is totally unique at 65 East, and each is a jewel of design, exhibiting choice materials from around the world.
Photograph courtesy of Fordham Company

Club 2700

Myefski Cook Architects

Even in the midst of enormous buildings, good design comes down to human scale. As Halsted Street carves its way north from the city, boutique storefronts at the base of traditional '4-flats' line the street creating a vibrancy that is supported by residents of the apartments and condominiums that rise above. In the heart of this Chicago thoroughfare, Club 2700 is designed to fit comfortably into this urban context with a careful crafting of massing and use of materials, but with a twist. Myefski Cook Architects came to the project and saw the opportunity for a great reminiscent building with a multidimensional architectural approach. The brick structure with its masonry detailing and limestone base is reminiscent of many of the surrounding buildings built after the turn of the century, while the interior provides seductive spaces that meet today's contemporary lifestyle.

FACING PAGE: Deep balconies create a strong articulation between the deliberately proportioned façades of the residential units, while providing great outdoor space for each resident.
Photograph by Chris Kelly Photography

Myefski Cook Architects designed Club 2700 from the ground-up on a site that accumulated seven city lots. Though this is a large five-story structure, the façade is purposely designed to appear as a series of smaller four-story components that emulate the proportion and scale of the neighborhood to bring it down to a pedestrian level. The solely retail first floor mirrors the adjacent buildings that have a commercial use for the first floor. To accentuate this first floor, Myefski Cook Architects employed a limestone base with horizontal reglets framing large glass openings between a series of articulated retail entrances. Not only does this first floor have 8,500 square feet of street-front retail, including a 6,000-square-foot spa, but it also has an inviting residential lobby and indoor parking that continues into a full parking garage beneath the entire building.

Counterbalancing the horizontal nature of the retail base, a tower element rises from the southern end of Club 2700, announcing the entrance to the residential spaces above. At its pinnacle the tower houses a hot tub adjacent to the common roof terrace, which affords spectacular views of the Chicago skyline. As a response to the street, the towers' roofs are curved, which metaphorically flows with traffic and draws attention to the building; this begins a motif of movement that continues inside.

LEFT: Vertical ribbons of masonry, glass and steel on the entry tower soar toward the sky, drawing the eye to the arched pinnacle.
Photograph by Chris Kelly Photography

FACING PAGE TOP: Arched screen clouds are backlit to diffuse light above the reception station, while daylight floods the lobby sitting area beyond.
Photograph by Chris Kelly Photography

FACING PAGE BOTTOM: The articulated fireplace and television niche punctuates the curved wall of the living room creating a dynamic form and functional focal point.
Photograph by Chris Kelly Photography

Curved forms draw residents and visitors through the entry space. The rounded reception station, made of a cherry veneer, has arcs of screen floating above like clouds that bring the scale from the high ceiling of the first floor down to human level. This use of curvature continues to the upper floors, making the units themselves more engaging. During the design process the total number of units in Club 2700 was reduced from 52 to 48 residences, providing a great opportunity to go more upscale. By combining what would have been the smallest units, the design team laid out units that are more exposed and open. Curved walls within each unit draw inhabitants through the space to the wonderful city views. While extremely dynamic in form these plans are also efficient, minimalist and affordable.

By employing curved forms and breaking up the façade, Myefski Cook Architects added a level of drama to a building that might have been overbearing as a more typical rectilinear structure. The redistribution of the massing also established to the community that large buildings do not necessarily overwhelm, but rather, as in the Club 2700, they may pleasantly augment a great neighborhood. ■ ■ ■ ■ ■ ■ ■ ■ ■ ■

Contemporaine

■ ■

Perkins + Will

■ ■ ■ ■ ■ ■ ■ ■ ■ Thanks in part to the elevator, residences in major cities have gone higher and higher into the sky. Thanks to Ralph Johnson of Perkins + Will, those high-rise residences are now not only functionally essential to big cities but also examples of fascinating art on a large frame. Contemporaine proves itself as a mesmerizing example of Chicago's progressive skyline and an example of what can be done with a little imagination and initiative.

Broken into two distinctive parts, Contemporaine seems to push up from the earth, the lower four levels offering parking and retail space. This garage base is opened with an all-glass wall system, which reveals animated ramps for the casual observer. These sloped ramps offer a respite for the otherwise rectilinear building, as great angles and movement mesmerize the eye. A narrow slot separates the base and tower, allowing essential transmission of the building systems, but that also voices a dialog between the building's two parts. Eleven stories above provide residential opportunities, supported

FACING PAGE: In its prime downtown site, Contemporaine has shifting masses to pose interesting architectural possibilities.
Project Design Team: Ralph Johnson, Bryan Schabel, Marius Ronnet and Curt Behnke.
Photograph by James Steinkamp Photography

by a 45-foot column—which is bookended with a matching rooftop column; these residences utilize floor-to-ceiling glass to allow for a high volume of natural light and to heighten views of downtown. Living spaces inside range from 950 to 2,700 square feet, and have natural wood flooring, while the roof offers some of the best views in the River North area of urban Chicago.

Exposure is taken to new levels at Contemporaine. Besides the open glass, the building features an unpainted concrete façade, with exposed structural elements, all of which lend themselves to an aesthetic education of the architectural process. As the building elevates, residential balconies cantilever, shooting out from the structure like catwalks. With 28 units, this coherent disorder allows for a balcony for each unit, which buttress Chicago's metropolitan vigor.

LEFT: At dusk, the heavy use of glass reveals a radiant core, while the structural positioning is unrivaled.
Photograph by James Steinkamp Photography

FACING PAGE TOP: Natural daylight floods the units. The floor-to-ceiling glass allows for great downtown views.
Photograph by James Steinkamp Photography

FACING PAGE BOTTOM: The sculptural quality of the roof deck proves that looking in is as aesthetically pleasing as looking out.
Photograph by James Steinkamp Photography

And though many condominiums offer one penthouse, Contemporaine has four from which to choose, featuring 20- to 32-foot glass walls.

Working under constraints, Ralph utilized tight spaces, restrictive budgets and multiple penthouses, producing an intriguing condominium that rejuvenates modern design. In 2005 the building won an Honor Award for Outstanding Architecture from the American Institute of Architects, and has received wonderfully positive feedback from *Chicago Tribune* and *The New York Times*. With Contemporaine, Perkins + Will proves itself yet again as an irreplaceable force in contemporary architecture, and proves Ralph as one of the finest building sculptors in today's market. ■ ■ ■ ■ ■ ■ ■ ■ ■ ■

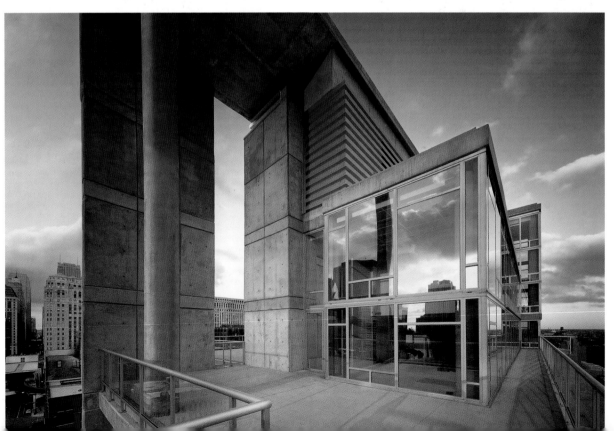

Erie on the Park

■ ■

Lucien Lagrange Architects

■ ■ ■ ■ ■ ■ ■ ■ ■ ■ Instincts play a great role in our lives, and many of the best decisions are made in those first few seconds. The door to the top penthouse at Erie on the Park was opened; a potential buyer then took a step inside and said, "I'll take it." Within seconds his deliberation was complete. The buyer could sense the elements that were put in place by Lucien Lagrange. For Lucien—an expert on instinctive construction—Erie on the Park became a task in creative design that flowed from the gut, in the face of what would otherwise seem impossible site constraints. But now Chicago has a fascinating residential tower as a result of Lucien's instincts.

FACING PAGE: Terraces provide expansive outdoor space and magnificent views of the Chicago skyline.
Project Design Team: Don Brown, Tim Hill, Lucien Lagrange, Wayne Miller and Margarita Retana.
Photograph by William Zbaren

To turn an impossibility into a positive, Lucien Lagrange Architects had to create a structure that was a direct response to a strange, acutely angled site. Lucien's client was not sure what to do with the site, but the architect understood that a striking shape could instill a sense of relative belonging to the building. By virtually chopping up the building, the designers were able not only to create fascinating penthouse terraces but also dynamic floorplans that are open and unique; as well, the disjointing enhances views to Lake Michigan, for terraces and balconies run up and down the 24-story building.

For this cul-de-sac site just off of Michigan Avenue, instinct suggested a very modern design. The structure is all steel, which means no interior columns, resulting in more open layouts. Erie on the Park utilizes revealed structure, and the recessed, 30-foot-high, glass-clad lobby and glass curtainwall add another dimension to the already remarkable geometry of the building. Steel and glass radiate as an image of a rough and strong structure. Tying in with the modern integrity is Erie on the Park's usable rooftop—a place for visions of large landscapes of the city skyline and the lake.

While the modernism in the building's stepped-back façade and exposed structure may evoke industrial sentiments, Erie on the Park is a great tie to the natural world. In addition to expansive views of both city and lake, the building is just a step away from a new, two-acre park and the Chicago River's River Walk. But, in its essence, this great parallelogram building is a prime example of how modern building and natural living can cohabitate in a practically seamless existence. Opened in 2002, Erie on the Park is now the architectural progeny of a cutting-edge city and a terrific addition to Lucien Lagrange Architects' oeuvre.

ABOVE: The building rises above light industrial red brick buildings near Yamasaki's famous former Montgomery Ward's headquarters a mile west of Chicago's Michigan Avenue high-rise buildings, adjacent to two parks, and near the Chicago River, giving prominence to the site.
Photograph by William Zbaren

RIGHT: The tower's form follows the 10,000-square-foot site's parallelogram shape, tucked between existing commercial buildings, sitting on abandoned railroad tracks.
Photograph by William Zbaren

FACING PAGE TOP LEFT: Cut-through openings in the cast-in-place concrete wall and glazing in the lobby link the masonry façades in the neighborhood with the building base.
Photograph by William Zbaren

FACING PAGE TOP RIGHT: The glass-walled lobby soars to 30 feet, creating an impressive vertical space rarely seen in residential projects.
Photograph by William Zbaren

FACING PAGE BOTTOM: Large, clear spans from the core to the exterior wall facilitated design freedom with 24 different open plans unencumbered by interior columns, including duplexes and expansive terraces.
Photograph by William Zbaren

The Fordham

■ ■

Fordham Company

■ ■ ■ ■ ■ ■ ■ ■ ■ ■ With each new development project, Fordham Company aspires to set new standards in high-rise residencies. For more than a

decade, the 20-year-old firm, headed by Christopher T. Carley, has developed exclusively in downtown Chicago. By focusing strictly on the high end, Fordham

Company is in a unique position to embed incomparable architecture into superb locations, while maintaining a strong focus on ambience and amenities.

This is truly the Fordham style, seen most deftly in East Superior Street's The Fordham, a major Chicago high rise that rediscovers the vintage residential building

for the new century. Fifty stories high, this statement in elegance is rare, for its ground-up build was specifically designed for residences of the highest stature

and design.

FACING PAGE: The penthouse at the 47th floor has some of the finest views north along the lake to Lincoln Park.
Photograph courtesy of Fordham Company

One of the tallest residential buildings in Chicago, The Fordham sits on the north side of town, just a few steps from Michigan Avenue. Sitting along a tree-lined street, The Fordham was a great opportunity for the developers, along with the esteemed architects of Solomon Cordwell Buenz, to design from the inside out. The developers and architects knew they wanted beautiful residences, but they let the homes dictate the design. In order to maximize views, shifting the tower's mass allowed for eight corners on every floor, a great aesthetic for the exterior and an interesting dynamic for the interior spaces. As the exclusive penthouses come into play, a series of setbacks cradles the residences inward, while metal gables cap the 50-foot-tall metal roof for a residential touch.

The amenities inside The Fordham are unstinted. While recessed balconies run throughout, each large residence has nine-foot ceilings, expansive windows that allow for better decorating around the frames and gas fireplaces that are highlighted alongside the custom cabinetry, granite countertops, marble and wood floor and elaborate moulding. For wine connoisseurs, there is individual storage in the 3,000-bottle wine cellar and tasting room, a humidor and lounge for smokers, a private movie theater, a spa and fitness center, a year-round pool and even a pet recreation area on the rooftop. And The Fordham also has that great, residential necessity for Chicago: stunning views in all directions.

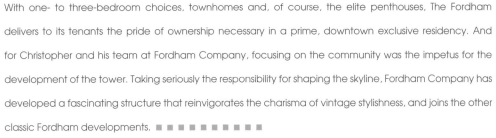

With one- to three-bedroom choices, townhomes and, of course, the elite penthouses, The Fordham delivers to its tenants the pride of ownership necessary in a prime, downtown exclusive residency. And for Christopher and his team at Fordham Company, focusing on the community was the impetus for the development of the tower. Taking seriously the responsibility for shaping the skyline, Fordham Company has developed a fascinating structure that reinvigorates the charisma of vintage stylishness, and joins the other classic Fordham developments. ■ ■ ■ ■ ■ ■ ■ ■ ■ ■

ABOVE LEFT: A custom dining room features rich bubinga paneling and dark walnut floors.
Photograph courtesy of Fordham Company

ABOVE RIGHT: Looking southwest at The Fordham, terraces, gables and dormers give it an unmistakable residential quality.
Photograph courtesy of Fordham Company

FACING PAGE TOP: The Fordham soars skyward from North Wabash Avenue; the corners and subtle angles maximize views.
Photograph courtesy of Fordham Company

FACING PAGE BOTTOM: The elegant penthouse master suites are heavily detailed in the woodwork, crown and casing.
Photograph courtesy of Fordham Company

The Heritage at Millennium Park

■ ■

Mesa Development, LLC
Walsh Investors, LLC

■ ■ ■ ■ ■ ■ ■ ■ ■ ■ In 2000, when the idea for The Heritage at Millennium Park was conceived, the land that was to become Millennium Park was a dusty railyard and a series of parking lots. It was hard to imagine the magnitude of the impact that Millennium Park would have as the construction of the urban park progressed. With iconic features like *Cloud Gate*—better known to Chicagoans as "The Bean"—*Crown Fountain* and the Frank Gehry-designed Jay Pritzker Pavilion, the park became more spectacular than anyone could have imagined. Chicago's Mesa Development and Walsh Investors had faith in the vision of Mayor Richard Daley and the city planners and assumed that the park would be successful. The firms were not disappointed. Now one of the top-rated destinations in the country, the Millennium Park neighborhood had to have spectacular residences to coincide with the park's imminent impact. The Heritage has become an icon in the postcard shot of Chicago's panorama.

FACING PAGE: The Heritage anchors the north end of the historic Michigan Avenue Street wall.
Photograph by David B. Seide, © Defined Space

Mesa Development and Walsh Investors assembled a one-acre site, comprised of seven separate parcels adjacent to the Chicago Cultural Center. Located in the heart of Michigan Avenue's Cultural Mile, residents of The Heritage enjoy easy access to world-class recreation, shopping and cultural venues. Symphony Center, The Art Institute of Chicago and the downtown theater district are only steps away. So are the boutiques of Chicago's two world-famous shopping districts: North Michigan Avenue and State Street.

The design challenge for Chicago-based architecture firm Solomon Cordwell Buenz was to design a building that offered incomparable views of Millennium Park, Grant Park, Lake Michigan and the famed Chicago skyline on a high-visibility location. Motion was key to the design, as Mesa Development did not want a flat building but rather one with undulating forms that would be in harmony with the artistic nature of the nearby park. Looking at The Heritage, one can see a gentle curvature to the structure with a selection of interacting colors—green, white and gold—to avoid a monochromatic sensation. The renovation of limestone, sandstone, brick and terracotta façades along historic Wabash Avenue creates a sublime classical effect. Large landscaped decks on the ninth and 28th floors of the tower coincide with not only the blue water of Lake Michigan but also the green space of Millennium Park. Due to the excellence of its design and its seamless integration into the famous Chicago skyline, The Heritage has become a prominent photographic opportunity for the millions of tourists who enjoy Millennium Park each year.

Despite the worldwide attraction of Millennium Park, a neighborhood feel is certainly reflected in The Heritage. Because of its classical exuberance and remarkable views of the park and the lake, The Heritage is recognized as one of the most successful luxury condominium developments in Chicago. It will be remembered as the iconic project that led the way in the creation of what is now Chicago's most popular residential neighborhood. ■ ■ ■ ■ ■ ■ ■ ■ ■

ABOVE LEFT: Beautiful vistas of Millennium Park and Lake Michigan are a highlight of The Heritage.
Photograph by David B. Seide, © Defined Space

ABOVE RIGHT: The new postcard view of Chicago is now complete.
Photograph by Richard P. Shields

FACING PAGE: The Heritage sits beyond the Millennium Monument, the park's peristyle.
Photograph by David B. Seide, © Defined Space

Lakeshore East

■ ■

Loewenberg Architects, LLC

■ ■ ■ ■ ■ ■ ■ ■ ■ ■ Rising in the heart of downtown Chicago, steps from such world-class attractions as Michigan Avenue, Millennium Park and Navy Pier, Lakeshore East spans 28 acres, believed to be one of the largest parcels of downtown land under development in a major United States city. This four-billion-dollar, mixed-use development in the rapidly growing New East Side neighborhood incorporates all the elements of a traditional city community, a lifestyle center that includes homes, retail, recreational opportunities and amenities such as a lush six-acre public park and a planned elementary school.

Prior to its transformation, the Lakeshore East site served as a transshipment port that supplied Chicago's growing economy in the mid-19th century, an Illinois Central railroad freight yard and, most recently, a par-three, nine-hole urban golf course.

FACING PAGE: Lakeshore East promises to be one of the most remarkable ventures in downtown living.
Photograph by David B. Seide, © Defined Space

It is also a place where master planners James Loewenberg, president of Loewenberg Architects and co-CEO of Magellan Development Group, and co-CEO of Magellan Development Group Joel Carlins are providing a forum for diverse architecture. Founded in 1919 by James's father and uncle, Lowenberg Architects has designed many of Chicago's premier planned communities. As architect of record, Loewenberg Architects knew that variety was a key to maximizing the distinctive location and proceeded to engage a number of world-class architects in a design collaboration that creates a preview of the future: a mixed-use development where people can live, work, shop, eat and pursue whatever interests them without having to get into a car. The plan that completes the ambitious Illinois Center development allows for the construction of up to 4,950 residences, a magnificent six-acre public park, 2.2 million gross square feet of commercial space, 1,500 hotel rooms, 400,000 square feet of retail space and a proposed elementary school.

FAR LEFT: Modern in design, yet classical in appeal, The Lancaster, which was the first residence completed in Lakeshore East, includes a glass curtainwall and pergola at the rooftop.
Photograph by David B. Seide, © Defined Space

LEFT: Drawing Lake Michigan up to the sky and soaring 87 stories, the fluid contour of Aqua's exterior is destined to be the most talked-about building in Chicago. The distinct residences offer a combination of Shore Club entertainment and recreational facilities with a host of indoor-outdoor options totaling 110,000 square feet.
Rendering by ImageFiction

FACING PAGE TOP: Loewenberg Architects' innovative design and technical expertise enhance the built environment and are witnessed throughout Chicago, including the exquisite lobby of The Regatta at Lakeshore East.
Photograph by Craig Skorburg

FACING PAGE BOTTOM: The magnificent park at Lakeshore East, designed by James Burnett and Chicago's Site Design Group, is the centerpiece of the community, blending green spaces and cascading fountains with a children's play park, a dog park and wireless internet access.
Photograph by Craig Skorburg

Among these projects is Aqua, a fascinating 82-story building, designed by Studio Gang Architects, with 670 units for condominium, rental and hotel use. Its curvilinear exterior functions along the continuing local metaphor of fluidity and motion—thanks to the river and the lake. Undulating concrete terraces, which extend up to 12 feet, destroy flatness and sterility, while ensuring uniqueness within unit floorplans.

Continuing Lakeshore East's modern design is The Lancaster, a 210-unit luxury condominium building, with a full-frontal glass exposure and unique rooftop terrace, designed by James and his team. Along with The Chandler, with its distinct façades, The Regatta, with its elliptical glass curtainwalls, The Shoreham, with its simple yet elegant structure, and The Tides, complete with varied balconies, Lowenberg Architects and Magellan Development Group have created a lifestyle community—a quiet, restful place that utilizes the natural occurrences of river and lake with panoramic views of Lake Michigan and a beautiful park down in the bowl of the parcel. While residents can walk to the business district of downtown, Lakeshore East is without a doubt a hidden gem, adjacent to the city core, and it successfully returns the majesty to this new Chicago neighborhood. ■ ■ ■ ■ ■ ■ ■ ■ ■ ■

Park Tower

Lucien Lagrange Architects

■ ■ ■ ■ ■ ■ ■ ■ ■ Like many of Lucien Lagrange's projects, Park Tower began with a phone call. The existing Park Hyatt Hotel, sitting in the heart of Chicago's Magnificent Mile, had some problems. Initially, the owners thought a rehab would be sufficient, for the 12 floors had fairly dreary architecture; but after a phone call with Lucien, they quickly found that they could expand vertically. This expansion would create a 200-room Park Hyatt hotel at the base, followed by high-end condominiums that shoot up 70 stories, fulminating into not only one of Chicago's tallest buildings but also one of its most intriguing.

FACING PAGE: Special attention was paid in construction to the circular formwork of the tower's load-bearing columns, creating a dramatic 30-foot lobby, featuring these four columns.
Project Design Team: Tim Hill, Lucien Lagrange and Wayne Miller.
Photograph by William Zbaren

There is no site in the world like Park Hyatt's 28,000-square-foot site. With great views down Michigan Avenue to the lake, and its proximity to Chicago's historic Water Tower—a survivor of the infamous fire—Lucien felt pushed to do something outstanding. The team began by taking down the old Park Hyatt, for the eight-foot ceilings were just not cutting it. Since this was to be the first high-end condos built in more than 20 years, Lucien wanted a special design; instead of being modern stylistically, with lots of sweeping glass planes, Park Tower ties to the history and context of Michigan Avenue, back to the quality of the 1920s—a more permanent structure with a little Art Deco injected.

There is softness to Park Tower as it rises 850 feet. Tinted windows alternate with structural columns clad in buff-colored limestone, a cool tone not often found on large buildings. Even the corners are slightly curved to mitigate some of the imposing stature of this vertical juggernaut. Inside, the designers added a foot of head space, which not only offers the strong mental calming effect of roominess, but also allows for the accommodation of oversized artwork. With formal interiors in the hotel, condos and retail spaces, Park Tower brings back a pre-WWII style almost forgotten since the modern movement began in the 1950s.

A building of Park Tower's size must always take note of swaying, especially in the Windy City. Strong winds can swing a skyscraper several feet, and to combat this, Lucien and his team hoisted a 300-ton tuned mass damper—a veritable pendulum—to combat that Chicago swing, which was the first of its kind installed during production. This damper sits above eight full-floor penthouses within a Park Tower exclusivity: a roof. The copper crown, while concealing the pendulum, contrasts the color forms of the building. But it also symbolizes that Park Tower is residential—a nice, comforting roof over occupant heads. ■ ■ ■ ■

ABOVE: All units have eastern lake exposures. Balconies and ceilings up to 15 feet high are other attractive design features.
Photograph by William Zbaren

RIGHT: With its tapering lines and multiple setbacks, the 67-story, 840,000-square-foot structure conveys an elegant and strong presence.
Photograph by William Zbaren

FACING PAGE TOP LEFT: The residential entrance features an intricate sunburst.
Photograph by William Zbaren

FACING PAGE TOP RIGHT: Park Tower is located in the heart of the Magnificent Mile, directly across a small street from Chicago's historic Water Tower of 1869, the iconic survivor of the great fire of 1870.
Photograph by William Zbaren

FACING PAGE BOTTOM: The top 57 stories are regarded by many as the city's finest condominium residences, among them eight full-floor penthouses. Views are spectacular, and always will be, because public park space extends from the building base to the shore of Lake Michigan, a half mile to the east.
Photograph by William Zbaren

River Village Pointe

Hirsch Associates LLC

For more than a century, Montgomery Ward sold city goods at country prices on its way to becoming an iconic Chicago retailer. In 2001 the company shut the doors to its historic campus along the north branch of the Chicago River. Given the area's prime location, riverside setting and beautiful historic structures, it did not take long for developers to create Kingsbury Park, a new neighborhood comprised of retail, residential and office uses in a combination of rehabbed buildings and new construction. As Kingsbury Park developed into a thriving urban neighborhood, one last site remained for redevelopment: an acute triangular parcel that would require some out-of-the-box thinking. In this unique spot, Hirsch Associates, along with developers The Enterprise Companies, created River Village Pointe.

FACING PAGE: From the south, River Village Pointe serves as a gateway to Kingsbury Park.
Photograph by Anthony May

In the midst of historic warehouse buildings, River Village Pointe brings a clearly modern expression into the urban fabric that is Kingsbury Park. Howard Hirsch, designer and principal of Hirsch Associates, looked to these neighboring buildings for clues that would allow a light-filled modern building to relate to the peculiarities of its site and the strength of its context, contrasting a horizontal banding of brick and limestone with a vertical expression of glass. Additionally, the unique triangular site allowed for some wonderful benefits: By expressing the acute corners with a glass curtainwall, Howard was able to maximize the views from within the units and maximize the visual impact of the building. Further emphasizing this corner, the design team canted up the roof, projected corner balconies and set back the first floor creating a Flatiron effect and a covered, pedestrian-scaled entry plaza.

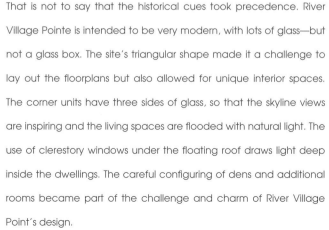

That is not to say that the historical cues took precedence. River Village Pointe is intended to be very modern, with lots of glass—but not a glass box. The site's triangular shape made it a challenge to lay out the floorplans but also allowed for unique interior spaces. The corner units have three sides of glass, so that the skyline views are inspiring and the living spaces are flooded with natural light. The use of clerestory windows under the floating roof draws light deep inside the dwellings. The careful configuring of dens and additional rooms became part of the challenge and charm of River Village Point's design.

River Village Point confirms that Hirsch Associates is a specialist in the design of urban infill developments. The firm's basic practices are so in tune with responsible urban building that the design incorporates affordable and CHA replacement housing into its unit mix. When LEED certification was sought for River Village Pointe, only a few minor tweaks enabled the effort. As the capstone to the Kingsbury Park project, River Village Pointe is the gateway to the new development and a fresh reading of old Chicago. ■ ■ ■ ■ ■ ■ ■ ■ ■ ■

ABOVE LEFT: A Flatiron effect sharpens the acute corner.
Photograph by Anthony May

ABOVE CENTER: The recessed entry provides a covered plaza while holding the corner.
Photograph by Anthony May

ABOVE RIGHT: River Village Pointe is a modern expression of its context, the historic masonry warehouse buildings of the Montgomery Ward campus.
Photograph by Anthony May

FACING PAGE LEFT: The Pointe penthouse has a sloped roof, clerestory windows and three walls of glass.
Photograph by Anthony May

FACING PAGE RIGHT: The Chicago skyline stands spectacular from a Pointe unit.
Photograph by Anthony May

Vetro

■ ■

Roszak/ADC

■ ■ ■ ■ ■ ■ ■ ■ ■ ■ The latest refined, light, diamond-like condominium building to emerge from Roszak/ADC is Vetro—"glass" in Italian. Sited in Chicago's South Loop-Printer's Row district, Vetro is one of a string of projects for which Thomas Roszak and his team served as developers, design-architects and construction managers. Since the firm has the great fortune of creating all its own projects, this terrific Chicago neighborhood, right near the river, would be blessed by one of the most fascinating condominium buildings around.

There are lots of ins and outs in Vetro's dynamic design. By shifting the 31-story mass, the Roszak team was able to enclose the first six floors in glass, so that parking became light and glowing by the use of translucent glass. This shifting creates a cantilever at the front entrance, which goes all the way to

FACING PAGE: Viewed looking up at the northwest corner, the building is a study of transparency, texture and reflectivity. Each extra corner provides residents more proprietary views. The parking level steps back at the seventh floor.
Project Design Team: Thomas Roszak, Tomoo Fujikawa, Jerry Johnson, Anna Simone and John Morley.
Photograph by Scott McDonald, Hedrich Blessing Photography

the street; as well, a landscaped terrace is created at the seventh floor, a great common space that not only affords wonderful views of the Chicago skyline but also has great spots for sunbathing or gathering, including a splash-pool. Level Seven is the magic common space, for residents may take yoga and Pilates classes in the workout rooms or step into the boutique spa for steam. Also in Vetro are plenty of social rooms for evening conferment.

Vetro was created with residents in mind. Minimizing residence hallways, the Roszak team designed for flowing spaces, which adds square footage but also leaves a very open feel to the units, which range from 550 to 2,400 square feet in 100-square-foot jumps. By recognizing the value in the European approach to more with less, the team brought in Toronto-based interior designer Anna Simone to refine the units. Rooms were amassed, widening spaces, and, because of the floor-to-ceiling glass, natural light is maximized and floods the units. Even the bedrooms are on the glass, for few things are more luxurious than waking to great city and lake views. With the best amenities, Vetro features exposed concrete ceilings and is laid out with wood floors and fine natural stone tile; all in Roszak/ADC's insistence on providing the best. At the streetscape a fountain and a light sculpture by world-acclaimed sculptor John David Mooney round out a complete package.

Built as an urban living product, Vetro is the next generation of building. Roszak/ADC demands quality construction, using appropriate high technology, hiring out the finest consultants in the market. With the addition of Vetro to the district, this once printing center of the Midwest is now one of the finest urban neighborhoods in Chicago. Just minutes away from all of the attractions that make Chicago what it is, Vetro is the new glass jewel on the block. ■ ■ ■ ■ ■ ■ ■ ■ ■ ■

ABOVE LEFT: Every fourth floor of the condos alternates with a deep, blue-tinted glass that organizes the building and refines the scale.
Photograph by Jon Miller, Hedrich Blessing Photography

ABOVE RIGHT: The lobby becomes a hotel-style living room. White, black and gray colors give a calm elegance to the space. The walls are painted Antarctica white and feature an alternating gloss/flat brick pattern.
Photograph by Scott McDonald, Hedrich Blessing Photography

FACING PAGE: The west elevation is a diagram showing 25 floors of residences perched atop six floors of parking enclosed in translucent glass. Two slender, 60-foot-tall columns perform a balancing act and seem to defy gravity by shifting the north edge toward Harrison Street.
Photograph by Scott McDonald, Hedrich Blessing Photography

CHAPTER THREE
City Projects

Many city treasures are housed in public spaces, including libraries, churches, government buildings and educational facilities—or perhaps these buildings themselves are the treasures. The excitement a weekly trip to the theater or the wonder a child feels stepping inside the cool interior of a museum surrounded by awe-inspiring works of art—these feelings are undeniably alive and guide the modern architects who commit their talents to these projects.

Whether the projects are entirely new, rehabilitative or for the purpose of historic preservation, there is a certain sense of grandeur and appropriateness that must be translated into the design plans—as is so eloquently exemplified in the Oriental Theatre by Daniel P. Coffey & Associates, Sullivan Center by Joseph Freed and Associates or the Wrigley Building by Powell/ Kleinschmidt and David Zeunert & Associates. Public spaces must reflect the city and the contemporary attitudes of its inhabitants while museums must delicately integrate facilities and engaging aesthetics for all ages.

No city project is without its own set of challenges, yet those challenges offer the opportunity to create public buildings and spaces where knowledge, resources and enjoyment are readily available for everyone from the young to the elderly. Enjoy a look into what designers are developing for these city institutions and gain rare insight into their thoughts and inspirations for their city through these projects.

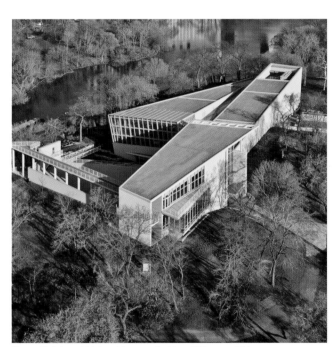

Peggy Notebaert Nature Museum, Perkins + Will, page 174

The Spertus Institute of Jewish Studies, Krueck & Sexton Architects, page 128

Museum of Science and Industry U-505 Submarine Exhibit, Goettsch Partners, page 162

The Spertus Institute of Jewish Studies

■ ■

Krueck & Sexton Architects

■ ■ ■ ■ ■ ■ ■ ■ ■ ■ Walk down Michigan Avenue and something becomes very clear: This face of Chicago carries all of the details and expressions of those who populate the city. Great architectural hands have touched this streetscape, from Burnham and Sullivan, to Holabird & Roche. Any new project stands on the shoulders of these giants; therefore, any new architectural statement here must communicate not only the mission of the building itself, but for the timeline of Chicago. The new Spertus Institute of Jewish Studies became that statement in 2007.

Light takes a central, metaphorical role in the Jewish tradition. When Spertus brought in Chicago's renowned Krueck & Sexton Architects, the design idea was to open the institute to the world, creating a transparency, something that would invite experience through its design, while utilizing light as the motif. The design team weaved this motif with the row of bay-filled buildings along Michigan Avenue—buildings defined by their movement. Wanting a very

FACING PAGE: The building's façade of folded glass planes reflects the vitality of the institute.
Photograph by William Zbaren

progressive design that reflected this undulation, the institute came alive with contemporary architecture through an abstract form of expression.

The initial design called for stone and glass, but Krueck & Sexton Architects soon realized that for light to be maximized and to come in a unique way, the 10-story, single-façade structure needed a glass wall. But this glass façade would not be flat. The Spertus Institute's face is created with 726 pieces of glass, cut into 556 shapes, and patterned into 39 different triangulated planes. This would-be glass canyon wall gives this midblock building dynamism virtually unseen before. As the glass ripples down the façade, a skirt at street level peels the institute's opening.

Careful steps were taken to connect people vertically once inside. The Spertus Institute is made of four different elements. There is a Jewish museum, two large libraries, a college—offering MAs and PhDs in Jewish studies—and a 400-seat auditorium for public programming, lectures and film. By cross-connecting the factions, Krueck & Sexton Architects opened up the floors, connecting people vertically as well as visually. By not containerizing these levels, the acoustics become a linking mechanism while there remains a distinct quietness.

LEFT: The entry skirt provides protection, expresses the entrance and reveals the detailing of the glass façade.
Photograph by William Zbaren

FACING PAGE LEFT: The building façade is a composition of openness and light.
Photograph by William Zbaren

FACING PAGE RIGHT: The folded, shimmering façade responds to the movement found on the historic Michigan Avenue streetwall.
Photograph by William Zbaren

As comfortably as The Spertus Institute sits among its neighbors, the design called for several special techniques to become neighborly in the environmental sense. Along with the water-saving fixtures, low-VOC materials combined with high-efficiency air filtration to enhance the building's performance. Special lighting—including the copious natural daylight that comes in—and other energy-saving mechanisms save a third of the building's energy consumption.

The Spertus Institute is a cultural building rather than a religious one—there are no overt Jewish symbols, in fact. The designers, therefore, wanted a structure that was culturally spirited. The public building—one of only a few with the good fortune of an esteemed Michigan Avenue address—wanted to be inviting, to encourage the public to come inside and explore the many dynamic treasures that the culture has to offer. And through a new, contemporary design, this 80-year-old institution can explore the timeless nature of learning through a fascinating architectural testimonial. ■ ■ ■ ■ ■ ■ ■ ■ ■ ■

TOP LEFT: The faceted wall of the building's 400-seat auditorium energizes the reception hall.
Photograph by William Zbaren

TOP RIGHT: The four-story atrium integrates the college, library and exhibitions floors.
Photograph by William Zbaren

BOTTOM LEFT: The ninth-floor great hall relies on skylights and light wells to bring natural light deep into the building.
Photograph by William Zbaren

FACING PAGE: A three-story reception hall elevates via a floating grand staircase.
Photograph by William Zbaren

850 Lake Shore Drive

Integrated Development Group
Booth Hansen
Interior Design Associates

■ ■ ■ ■ ■ ■ ■ ■ ■ 850 Lake Shore Drive was built in the Roaring Twenties by one of the country's greatest turn-of-the-century architects, Jarvis Hunt. The building's Classical Revival architectural style was the perfect setting for its original use as the Lake Shore Athletic Club. The 17-story building, located at the forefront of the Streeterville neighborhood and adjacent to the famed Gold Coast, is just two blocks from Chicago's premier shopping district, the Magnificent Mile. Once the site of the 1928 Olympic trials, the Lake Shore Athletic Club was purchased by Northwestern University in the 1970s and converted into graduate law and medical student housing. When Northwestern decided to sell the building, a Chicago icon and an irreplaceable piece of the city's skyline, local opposition to the demolition mounted and spurred Integrated Development Group to seize the opportunity to adaptively reuse the building.

FACING PAGE: Originally the Lake Shore Athletic Club, 850 Lake Shore Drive will be adaptively reused and developed into a boutique luxury senior living community.
Project Design Team: Matthew K. Phillips, Laurence Booth, Harry Soenksen and Bonnie B. Manson.
Photograph by William Zbaren

Integrated Development Group's mission is to create the "next generation of luxury senior living." The ultimate goal is to design a building imperceptible as a senior living community. When Matthew Phillips, President and CEO of Integrated Development Group, learned of Northwestern's intention to sell 850 Lake Shore Drive, he immediately recognized the opportunity to preserve Hunt's masterpiece and create a boutique senior living community for Chicagoans who desire to remain downtown.

The building's premier lakefront location will afford future residents and their guests spectacular views of not only Lake Michigan but also Chicago's skyline. In designing the vast array of community areas, the architects have consulted Hunt's original plans, so as not to be influenced by the building's most recent use. Lead architect Laurence Booth believes 850 Lake Shore Drive presents an incredible opportunity to demonstrate how "tradition and innovation belong together in design." Two of the premier community areas will be the Grand Salon and Club Room, spaces included in Hunt's original design. The classic character of these existing spaces will be combined with modern innovations while maintaining their elegance and spirit. Current plans also call for green roofs to be created, providing outdoor space for residents and their guests to enjoy, while being environmentally conscious.

TOP LEFT: The Club Room, which features hand-carved, ornately detailed millwork, overlooks Lake Michigan and will be a social gathering space for future residents. Photograph by William Zbaren

BOTTOM LEFT: Exquisite, hand-crafted decorative plaster mouldings accent the Grand Salon with magnificent views of Lake Michigan. The Grand Salon will be the senior living community's formal dining room. Photograph by William Zbaren

The traditional design of the community areas will be continued through the 128 independent living and 11 assisted living residences. High-end finish levels found throughout the common areas will be carried through to the residences with top-of-the-line appliances and materials. At 1,650 square feet, the average square footage of the independent living residences is significantly larger than other senior living communities. The design and size of these residences will allow future 850 Lake Shore Drive residents to downsize from their current home while not downsizing their lifestyle.

The breath of new life Integrated Development Group is providing will return 850 Lake Shore Drive to its heyday. In the spirit of Hunt's original design, this architectural treasure will achieve a restored architectural experience and enduring quality for its next generation of residents. ■ ■ ■ ■ ■ ■ ■ ■ ■ ■

ABOVE LEFT: 850 Lake Shore Drive's limestone and terracotta façade is Classical Revival in style.
Photograph by William Zbaren

ABOVE RIGHT: The chandelier in the Grand Salon is one of the many original elements being utilized in the interior design.
Photograph by William Zbaren

ABLA/Fosco Community Center

Nia Architects, Inc.

■ ■ ■ ■ ■ ■ ■ ■ ■ ■ Five minutes west of downtown Chicago, a little community was selected for a new building by the Public Building Commission of Chicago. The vision for this center was to bring in several public agencies to set up nonprofit facilities under one roof, intending to reinvigorate this Chicago community. Anthony Akindele of Nia Architects had been established with the PBC, through various projects, prior to opening his own firm. Because of this history, PBC knew that Anthony had the capacity to develop a community building that could prioritize athletics, daycare, after-school classes, while featuring a pool and refurbished fields, and still work within a budget.

ABLA/Fosco is comprised of a childcare center with stimulating indoor-outdoor spaces for childhood education, as well as multipurpose classrooms for after-school learning, adult education, hands-on job training and computer learning. The facility also has indoor and outdoor playgrounds for kids, as

FACING PAGE: A southwest view of the main entry plaza highlights the thoughtful landscaping.
Project Design Team: Anthony Akindele, Paul Effanga, Bruce Blair, Clemenstein Love and Gary Jung.
Photograph by Dan Machnik

well as an intense gymnasium, a fully equipped fitness center and an indoor swimming pool that boasts a high, curved ceiling with walls of windows to inspire active lifestyles.

Beyond its educational and recreational spaces, ABLA/Fosco was designed with many other factors in mind to make it an inviting, innovative, easily accessible and safe place for everyone. The openness of the center welcomes—the clerestory in the central space proves an airy summons for the public, while the linear design and landscaped plaza nestle the building into nature's hold. As well, energy efficiency was achieved through the use of low-E, double-glazed windows and roof assemblies with high R-values. Clerestories were employed to admit additional natural light, while a large expanse of energy-efficient glazing further reduces the building's dependency on artificial light.

TOP LEFT: The workout room has modern equipment.
Photograph by Dan Machnik

BOTTOM LEFT: Because of its western exposure, the gymnasium receives diffused light. The bleachers are retractable.
Photograph by Dan Machnik

FACING PAGE TOP: The interior swimming pool utilizes a queen-post roof structure and south-facing curtainwall system.
Photograph by Dan Machnik

FACING PAGE BOTTOM: During the summer months, children explore the outdoor water feature at the west façade.
Photograph by Dan Machnik

The modern center arrives with perfect timing. Because the neighborhood had been neglected, the building brightens lives inside a structured environment, as a beacon for a community that has not seen replenishing construction in years. As well, the east side, around Racine Street, is a fresh area in the process of being gentrified. For Anthony, the project proved a link between old and new Chicago, and revealed fresh possibilities in youth-centered building.

Anthony was born and raised in Nigeria, and the word "Nia" is a word for "purpose." Anthony's design heads for one goal: to beautifully embody its purpose. Utilizing the latest technology available, Nia Architects' designs have unquestionable clarity and an unmistakable attention to detail. This is evident in that ABLA/Fosco Community Center is in plans to be replicated throughout neighborhoods in Chicago. ■ ■ ■ ■ ■ ■ ■ ■ ■

Armenian Evangelical Church of Chicago

Arzoumanian & Company

■ ■ ■ ■ ■ ■ ■ ■ ■ ■ Although building a new house of worship in a Chicago suburb may not seem like a particularly momentous or historic occurrence, there is more to the design and construction of the Armenian Evangelical Church of Chicago in Mount Prospect, Illinois, than meets the eye. Dedicated in 2007, the new structure is the first new Armenian church in the Midwest in more than two decades, built for one of the 10 oldest congregations in the Armenian Evangelical Union of North America. For most of its 90-year history, the congregation occupied one of the few remaining large houses on North Sheridan Road in Chicago, and so the joy of finally having the means to construct a new home specifically for its needs is very much the answer to a prayer.

The design for the new structure, however, needed to reflect both the 1,700-year-old Orthodox roots of the Armenians as the first Christian nation, and the congregation's contemporary evolution as a western Protestant denomination founded by American missionaries in the mid-19th century.

FACING PAGE: The layered façade creates a symbolic interplay of old and new. Fourth-century Armenian script over the entry doors is superseded by the contemporary Western identity of the congregation.
Photograph by Patsy McEnroe

In style and mass, Raffi Arzoumanian, AIA, NCARB, strove to create a contemporary interpretation of Armenia's distinctive religious architecture, which dates back to the fourth century and which is widely regarded as one of the forerunners of the great cathedrals of Europe. At the same time, economics demanded that all materials be readily available and that the general contracting be managed by Fred Simonian, a member of the parish who is a retired chemical engineer. Red brick façades, reminiscent of the burnt sienna tones of the native "touf" stone of Armenia, are highlighted with contrasting bands of limestone, employing a traditional decorative effect of the ancient structures. The mountainous terrain of Armenia is reflected in a prominent front wall concealing a porte-cochere flanked by two towers capped by an ornamental dome, which creates a trinity of building masses that gives the entire building additional prominence from the street. An archway cut into the façade frames a stately double-doored entrance. Inside, the calm and simple sanctuary interior is dignified by a series of vaulted ceilings. A sloped floor and a central arch capped with an inscription in the traditional Armenian manner focus all attention on the pulpit and a backlit stained glass window depicting a praying Jesus Christ.

In the rear of the building, a commercial kitchen and multipurpose hall give the congregation great flexibility to use the community gathering space for social and educational events and programs. ■ ■ ■ ■ ■ ■ ■ ■ ■ ■

TOP LEFT: Borrowing from his experience in designing performance spaces, Raffi Arzoumanian gave the sanctuary a sloped floor to better focus attention and improve sight lines toward the pulpit.
Photograph by Patsy McEnroe

BOTTOM LEFT: Tablets flanking the central arch of the façade are inscribed with a Biblical verse and a testament to the Armenian Genocide of 1915.
Photograph by Patsy McEnroe

FACING PAGE: The church's twin towers and ornamental dome are reminiscent of Armenia's mountainous terrain and historical architecture. The broad porte-cochere creates a grand entryway.
Photograph by Patsy McEnroe

Bloomingdale's and Tree Studios

Daniel P. Coffey & Associates, Ltd.

■ ■ ■ ■ ■ ■ ■ ■ ■ ■ Despite being listed by the World Monuments Fund as a key landmark for preservation, the Bloomingdale's and Tree Studios building was once threatened with demolition. Daniel P. Coffey, FAIA, was urgently requested to develop concepts for adaptive reuse and preservation that might prevent this demolition so that the owners could recoup the same land value as a 40-story condominium.

With Daniel's reuse concept and the bold combination of resources from the City of Chicago, Friedman Properties and Federated Department Stores—Bloomingdale's—a public-private partnership was established that allowed the owners, the Shriners, to achieve full value on the sale of the property.

FACING PAGE: An overall view of Medinah Temple/Bloomingdale's reveals the restored onion domes and new signage, corner entries and enlarged storefronts. Photograph by James Steinkamp Photography

The landmark properties had been both an auditorium and headquarters for the Shriners on the east and an artist colony with retail shops on the west. This circa-1910 auditorium, known as the Medinah Temple, was styled in the likeness of a romanticized Islamic mosque. The interior was rather plain, but the exterior, though deteriorated, was a dynamic mix of heavy masonry, stained glass and touches of Islamic terracotta detailing. The building had always been well known for its exotic exterior and as the annual home of the Shriners' Circus. This pairing of memories formed an important basis for the outcry for preservation.

The adjacent two- and three-story Tree Studios, circa 1890, is subtler in its original architecture and even more deteriorated. Lovingly restored to museum-quality preservation, the building now houses various boutique establishments that have enhanced the streetscape and shopping just off Magnificent Mile. However, the magic of Tree Studios lies in its smaller, two-story scale and the quiet, oasis-like landscaped courtyard.

By contrast, the huge auditorium had no ability to create economic value as it was. The reuse concept suggested that a redevelopment method would need to dismantle the interior floors and balconies, dig a deeper basement and slip a new building into the old walls, roof and ceiling. This became a four-level, 150,000-square-foot Bloomingdale's.

This mammoth undertaking preserved the landmark exterior with its massive, brown masonry and inserted a bright, white, airy, modern store that centers on an interior atrium, topped by the original plaster-domed ceiling. The new structure seems to float within the glowing, stained glass windows and old masonry walls. With an array of spotlighting, the effect is an excellent presentation of

merchandise rivaling any art museum. On the exterior, a pair of long-lost copper onion domes has been replaced, while subtle signage and lighting have been added, making it clear that this is a very special place in the city.

The transition from exterior to interior, from massive to spacious, from dark to light, is magical, and the uncovering of original plaster elements from column capitals to magnificent ceiling coffers and domes, coupled with the wonderful stained glass windows, allows an enlightening process of architectural discovery as one moves through the store. ■ ■ ■ ■ ■ ■ ■ ■ ■ ■

ABOVE LEFT: With new windows and terraces for offices, Tree Studios is separated from the Medinah Temple by a restored courtyard.
Photograph by Barbara Karant

ABOVE RIGHT: The main entrance to Bloomindale's contrasts the refurbished canopy with a glimpse of the bright, white interior.
Photograph by Ballogg Photography

FACING PAGE TOP LEFT: The new Bloomingdale's atrium is beneath the restored dome, with a proscenium and drape in the background.
Photograph by Hedrich Blessing Photography

FACING PAGE TOP RIGHT: The open floorplan layout cascades down multiple floors.
Photograph by Hedrich Blessing Photography

FACING PAGE BOTTOM: Tree Studios was restored to its original, 19th-century condition.
Photograph by Barbara Karant

Christian Life Center

■ ■

McBride Kelley Baurer

■ ■ ■ ■ ■ ■ ■ ■ ■ A successful church should offer a feeling of connection and fellowship for its congregation. The Moody Church wanted a stronger sense of community for its new Christian Life Center. The church's sanctuary gracefully seats more than 3,000 people, yet in the rest of the facility, there were no places to connect, no spaces for large gatherings—no room to grow.

McBride Kelley Baurer was challenged with designing an addition to one of the largest Romanesque structures in the United States. Would the team pull features of the original design or contrast them? They decided that they would not simply mimic the original architecture. The plan was to design in character, invoking the same carefulness of the antecedent structure, blending details for a contemporary version with ties to the original.

FACING PAGE: From Clark Street, The Moody Church addition is a seamless transition for the Romanesque structure.
Project Design Team: Keith Criminger, Janet Chu, Bruce Roth, Greg Battoglia and Adam St. Cyr.
Photograph by Ballogg Photography

The features include similar red brick utilized on the Clark and LaSalle façades. Yellow-tinted terracotta capitals relate to existing terracotta details from the older building. Grand arched windows function as both blending elements and openings for natural light. But the addition is also different. The original rooms were not bright and airy due to thick masonry exterior walls and multiple interior columns. So MKB designed the addition to have large, virtually column-free spaces, along with glass curtainwall systems to lighten the interior. There is a new roof deck at the third floor of the Christian Life Center with a curved glass wall and wonderful views of Lincoln Park across the street. A larger roof deck on top of the addition includes a green roof surrounding a terrace for outdoor gatherings.

Most urban churches have minimal large-scale spaces for gathering or events. The key planning feature here was to create more openness and a variety of places for attendees to connect with each other. The first floor has an enlarged lobby, multiple seating areas and expandable classrooms, which can accommodate gatherings of several hundred people. The second floor is dedicated to Children's Ministry, with a library and an expanded nursery. The third floor has adult fellowship rooms, a café area and access to the enviable gathering spaces on the roof decks.

Through the process of master planning, McBride Kelley Baurer assists mission-oriented organizations, like The Moody Church, to balance immediate needs with long-term goals. The Christian Life Center exemplifies the value of this process and creates a beautiful and functional new addition that will benefit many generations of The Moody Church family. ■ ■ ■ ■ ■ ■ ■ ■ ■ ■

ABOVE LEFT: Style and comfort played heavy roles in the design of the church's reception lobby.
Photograph by Ballogg Photography

ABOVE RIGHT: The floor-and-ceiling pattern continues in this third-floor seating area.
Photograph by Ballogg Photography

FACING PAGE TOP: One of the church's new features is a third-floor café.
Photograph by Ballogg Photography

FACING PAGE BOTTOM: The second-floor Children's Ministry takes a playful turn in its design.
Photograph by Ballogg Photography

Evanston Fire Station #3

■ ■

Yas Architecture, LLC

■ ■ ■ ■ ■ ■ ■ ■ ■ Many children dream of becoming a firefighter. While fighting flames certainly calls noble images to mind, the actual day-to-day job of a firefighter includes a lot of downtime as they calmly await an emergency call.

Evanston Fire Station #3 was in disrepair and needed to update to current ADA codes. When the original station was designed, the rank-and-file were not consulted, resulting in a space that did not provide convenient or practical use of the facility. There was no privacy for the crew, and the dormitory-style bunk room required bed-sharing over the three shifts.

FACING PAGE: The front elevation of Evanston Fire Station #3 shows the merging of contrasting materials.
Project Design Team: Stephen Yas, Jonathan Fischel, Joseph Macneil, Tim Bennett, Krista Simons-Gliva and Michael Thompson.
Photograph by Chris Barrett, Hedrich Blessing Photography

Stephen Yas, AIA, RIBA, of YAS Architecture—formerly Yas/Fischel Partnership—was chosen for this project based on his design process and methodology. Working closely with the city personnel and the fire station staff, Stephen designed a new building on the existing narrow, triangular-shaped site. In an effort to truly understand the requirements of the firefighters within their space, Stephen spent time at the station, hanging out with the firefighters and listening to their stories. By doing this he was able to create a practical and well-designed fire station that met the needs of the firefighters who serve the City of Evanston.

He started by giving them comfort. Each firefighter per shift gets his or her own room and individual bed. The new station has a physical fitness area, flat screen televisions and recliner chairs. The new great room was given a residential atmosphere and a gourmet kitchen was installed, since kitchens are high priorities in firefighter's lives. The result is a building that is truly of the firefighters.

Rather than typical brick, Stephen chose a checkerboard pattern for the exterior masonry to symbolize the diversity of the firefighters. The apparatus bays are south-facing glass and use passive-solar to reduce the energy requirement. They open to reveal the highly polished engines within, a shrine to these works of art that protect the community. The station's tower is reminiscent of the traditional hose-drying towers and houses the shift commander, giving him a view of the street and apparatus bay entrances in both directions. A spotlight shines upward at night to illuminate the flag as a remembrance to the firefighters at Ground Zero. Additionally, a white and a red light are left on the building exterior as a modern interpretation of the horse-drawn-carriage era of firefighting.

Evanston Fire Station #3 has become a prototype for the modern fire stations in the area. Designing with function, as well as compassion, YAS Architecture developed a structure for the people—those inside, in uniform, and those outside, in the community. ■ ■ ■ ■ ■ ■ ■ ■ ■ ■

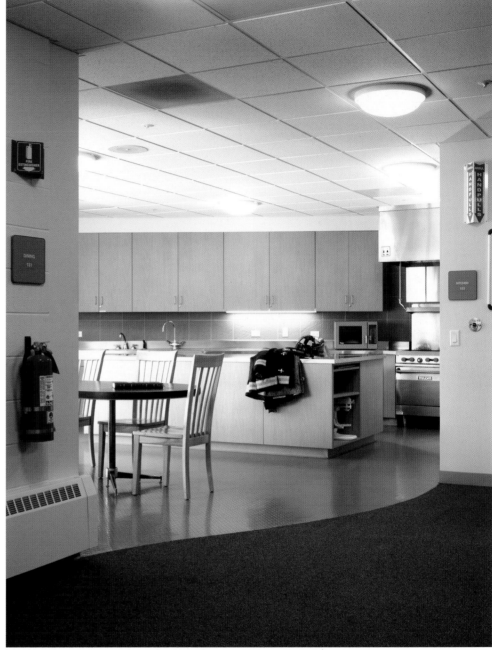

ABOVE LEFT: The apparatus room has large glass doors to open the trucks to the public.
Photograph by Chris Barrett, Hedrich Blessing Photography

ABOVE RIGHT: A hotspot in any fire station, the kitchen is designed for heavy use.
Photograph by Chris Barrett, Hedrich Blessing Photography

FACING PAGE: The station's tower is reminiscent of the old hose-drying towers, and functions as a beacon for the town.
Photograph by Chris Barrett, Hedrich Blessing Photography

Grace Church

■ ■

Ethos Workshop

■ ■ ■ ■ ■ ■ ■ ■ ■ ■ Grace Church sits in the northern Chicago suburb of Wheeling. This evangelical, Korean congregation had quickly grown out of its existing space, as such things seem to happen with churches—the power to draw people in has the occasional fateful side effect of thinning elbow room. Scott Allman, AIA, of Ethos Workshop became aware of the church's desire to build a new facility, and soon he was brought in to design a building that would serve their future needs. His solution was a simple, modern structure that had humble character, but that had very specific purposes in mind.

How does one design a building that portrays spiritual overtones without being overly liturgical? Scott spent time getting to know the congregation, finding out the specifics of its assembly. Since Grace Church is predominantly Korean, imbibing some of the Korean traditions was a primary driving force. However, it became evident that the building needed to harmonize the church's multiple generations. While many in the congregation are native

FACING PAGE: From the exterior, a theme of division, and inevitable collaboration, is developed between the major wings.
Photograph by Mike Crews, Crews Photography

Koreans, a good portion are American-born and, subsequently, westernized. The building's design had to facilitate one church body that functions as two, often independent, congregations under one roof, accommodating multiple generations—and languages.

Separated into three distinct volumes, the building looks little like a traditional church. The 450-seat sanctuary is clad in red brick, while the offices and classrooms are housed behind a contrasting wall of stone panels. A multipurpose gymnasium and kitchen sit in the rear, while all three volumes are connected by a central glass atrium. On the second floor of the classroom wing, a 250-seat chapel exists beyond a series of vertical windows that form part of a cross image. Film on the windows allows the color to change with the seasons, like an ever-evolving stained glass window, which allows for interesting nuances of interior light. To very tangibly bring in the traditional Korean culture, a selection of the building's materials was shipped from Korea, including the prominent stainless steel cross standing by the church's front door.

Although the building is designed to accommodate multiple, simultaneous worship activities, the entire congregation meets for a traditional meal once a week in one of the new building's assembly areas. Finding these core values of the clients—such as Grace's congregation—is where Ethos Workshop thrives. Scott remains ever interested in discovering the relationship between a building and the culture it is intended to represent. Because of the church's penchant for overgrowth, this design intentionally provided for the possibility of future additions. Which, for Grace Church, might be sooner rather than later. ■ ■ ■ ■ ■ ■ ■ ■ ■

TOP RIGHT: Many of the materials were shipped from Korea, including the steeple.

BOTTOM RIGHT: The front entrance enforces the nexus that symbolically unifies the church's dichotomy.

FACING PAGE: From the main worship space, the congregation can see Grace Church's frontage windows that are laced with a seasonably changeable, colored film. Photographs by Mike Crews, Crews Photography

Museum of Science and Industry
U-505 Submarine Exhibit

■ ■

Goettsch Partners

■ ■ ■ ■ ■ ■ ■ ■ ■ Ask any 10-year-old boy: There is nothing sweeter than an enormous submarine. Thanks to the efforts of Goettsch Partners and the Museum of Science and Industry, we can all step into the wet shoes of Captain Nemo and experience, safely, one of the war effort's most interesting phenomena: U-505.

Historically, U-505 was not a friendly, as they say. This German U-boat was captured off the coast of Africa—its rudder crushed by Allied depth charges, its mechanical systems on the fritz and a whole lot of water coming in. The submarine surfaced and the Nazi crew surrendered. From within, the Allies found critical codebooks—the Holy Grail for our cryptanalysts.

FACING PAGE: The design of the new exhibit space recalls World War II-era submarine pens and dry docks, with exposed concrete walls and arched steel girders.
Project Design Team: Michael F. Kaufman, Leonard Koroski, Michael Heider, William Boznos and Jeffrey Johnson.
Photograph by Jon Miller, Hedrich Blessing Photography

For years the submarine was moved around, until it reached Chicago and was put on display as a museum exhibit. Exposed to the elements, U-505 was losing its skin. The consensus was that without protection, the sub was lost. So, in 2005, U-505 submerged once again—this time in earth.

Goettsch Partners created what is essentially a bathtub underneath the front lawn of the Museum of Science and Industry. This colossal waterproof enclosure has splayed walls to both support the vast amount of earth forces and to create perspective. This giant containment unit interprets the militaristic design elements of World War II submarine pens.

Once the holding elements were in place, the next step was to move the U-boat. Setting this fragile, 700-ton behemoth atop 12 wheeled, motorized dollies, the crew took three days getting the boat in place. Once inside, the crew sealed the top with a curved structure and covered the whole with grass—rendering the exhibit completely invisible from the surface level.

TOP LEFT: Neatly concealed beneath the museum's front lawn, the submerged exhibit leaves the view of the 1893 museum completely unobstructed and preserves the historic landscape plan.
Photograph by Steinkamp/Ballogg Photography

BOTTOM LEFT: Interactive displays and historic photographs are tucked underneath a gradually descending ramp and cantilevered viewing platforms.
Photograph by Jon Miller, Hedrich Blessing Photography

FACING PAGE: The space allows the sub to take center stage, reinforcing the imposing image of the U-505 and giving visitors a true sense of its place in history.
Photograph by Steinkamp/Ballogg Photography

It was important to create movement around the submarine. Using very simple precast structures as walking paths allowed for moveable display areas below, so that the flow around the boat can be maximized at all times. Creating safe, easy access to this submerged exhibit required digging tunnels from the museum's existing building, which required very careful work on the design team's part because of the existing Columbian Exposition building's foundations.

The response has been incredible. So much anticipation was built from the very public move of this World War II icon that the design team was able to work with other area firms who were facing similar adjacent underground problems with the reconstruction of Lake Shore Drive. The build, in other words, was a public affair; and the people of Chicago can take ownership of this structurally functional yet extremely exciting addition to the United States museum culture.

Oriental Theatre

■ ■

Daniel P. Coffey & Associates, Ltd.

■ ■ ■ ■ ■ ■ ■ ■ ■ ■ Originally built in the mid-1920s as a movie palace, with occasional vaudevillian acts and music, Oriental Theatre had been abandoned after a decade as an exploitation film venue. It had deteriorated significantly and the vacant auditorium evoked Indiana Jones' "Temple of Doom."

Now, it is a beautifully adapted and expanded world-class venue. The motivation to reclaim the venue for modern use came via the planning leadership of Daniel P. Coffey, FAIA. His North Loop Theatre District Revitalization Planning efforts were undertaken in conjunction with City of Chicago, State Street Council and the Chicago Central Area Committee efforts to make Chicago's Loop a dynamic and exciting, 24/7 environment. Oriental Theatre sits in the heart of the new district between three other venues adapted and put back into use by Daniel—The Chicago and Palace Theatres and the Gallery

FACING PAGE: The ornate auditorium hides the heavy restoration.
Photograph by James Steinkamp Photography

37 Center for the Arts. These anchor the largest and most dynamic theater district outside London and New York. A phone call by Daniel to a prominent Toronto theatrical producer started the venture. Three years later, it was a grand opening night at the Oriental.

The stage expansion was a mammoth undertaking that involved remarkable structural engineering and construction coordination. The eight-story, Oliver Building façade was temporarily held up while a two-story basement excavation for dressing rooms, stage trap and rehearsal facilities was accomplished. The resultant stage doubled in size and depth. With the insertion of a pair of 60-foot-long transfer trusses to carry a stage-obstructing column from the adjacent 22-story Oriental Office Tower, this made for a complex and costly, but necessary, construction project.

As the stage and its support spaces are the engine that makes a theatrical venue function, the producer/owner of the facility knew that with the new stage, the venue could become a very special theater.

Oriental Theatre was originally a very tight, 3,000-seat venue with minimal stage, dressing room, toilet, concessions and lobby space. It also had no handicapped accessibility. The vast number and degree of changes undertaken to make the facility state-of-the-art are seamless. The nearly all-new facility looks as if it all dates back to its original opening night.

Yet it now has just fewer than 2,300 wider, more spaciously arrayed seats that are served by two rather than five aisles. The sightlines were gently improved by raising parts of the main floor. The rear walls of the main level were pulled in about five rows and the area converted to lobby expansion and concession/

merchandise areas. The basement was totally reconstructed for both support spaces and ample, new restrooms. A V.I.P. entertainment suite and a handicapped-accessible elevator were carefully integrated. The fire-destroyed upper lobbies were recreated, as were the new exterior marquee and vertical sign. The main floor lobby had been an electronics store for 15 years. Now, it is an inviting box office and entrance to this magically restored theater. ■ ■ ■ ■ ■ ■ ■ ■ ■ ■

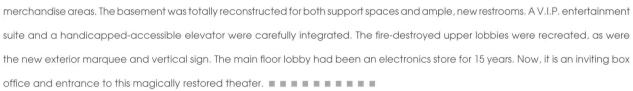

ABOVE LEFT: From the balcony, the restored lobby overlooks the mezzanine.
Photograph by James Steinkamp Photography

ABOVE RIGHT: Detail work in the lobby shows a deft hand, as the new concession sits within.
Photograph by James Steinkamp Photography

FACING PAGE: The new marquee and vertical sign recall the old theater days.
Photograph by James Steinkamp Photography

The Park at Lakeshore East

■ ■

Site Design Group, Ltd.

■ ■ ■ ■ ■ ■ ■ ■ ■ ■ The new 28-acre Lakeshore East site sets the bar for urban development. Positioned now among the tallest buildings in not only Chicago but the United States, this area was a bustling rail hub in the 1800s, significantly redefined by the Great Chicago Fire of 1871. As fire debris allowed for eastward expansion immediately following this historic event, only recently has the final portion of the original railroad parcel been realized. At the heart of the 28-acre development lies The Park at Lakeshore East, a six-acre green space that balances the built form of the developing neighborhood. Chicago's Site Design Group led the management team to develop this great addition to the city's venerable park system.

ABOVE: Children delight at the colorful and interactive playground at the park.
Photograph by Ron Gordon

FACING PAGE: Bold colors and geometric forms highlight the playground component of Lakeshore East.
Project Design Team: Ernest C. Wong and Michelle M. Inouye.
Photograph by Ron Gordon

Under the masterplanning of Skidmore, Owings & Merrill and the office of James Burnett, the park was designed around two sweeping terraces, mimicking the boat sails a block away in Lake Michigan. Collaborating further with the office of James Burnett, Site Design Group pushed for a landscape with bold forms that utilize traditional materials through a more modern expression. Access to the park is directed and controlled at key locations through the use of clearly identified entry paths. A grand staircase at the south capitalizes on the site's significant grade change, and a strong series of seatwalls punctuate the lower north plaza. The east and west entries accommodate vertical connections associated with the surrounding buildings.

Dual water terraces organize the main park zones. A series of five basins, each lined with rugged black boulders, provides a deep, richly textured water surface that allows for continuous interest when the fountains are drained for the winter months. A central open space functions for both active and passive uses and organizes the more intimate park spaces. A dog-friendly area and the playground offer great incentives for outdoor activities for Lakeshore East residents. Families of site furnishings and lighting, pavement material and color choices, and the rich variation of Lannon stone, granite, cedar wood and metals meld into contemporary forms to provide a unique park space.

TOP LEFT: The path's sweeping design leads visitors through every area of the park.
Photograph by Ron Gordon

TOP RIGHT: The cascading stairwell serves as the ground entrance into this spectacular space.
Photograph by Ron Gordon

BOTTOM LEFT: The fountains entertain visitors of all ages.
Photograph by Ron Gordon

FACING PAGE: The pools of water capture the tranquility of this urban park at night.
Photograph by Ron Gordon

There is something truly fascinating about a passive open space within the urban fabric, for parks are the microcosms of the neighborhood. A green oasis in a bowl of towering structures propels something meditative from any perspective. Due to this integral effect, the park had the fortune of winning the 2002 AIA Urban Design Award, doing as much justice for the built world as its neighbor, Lake Michigan, has done for the natural. Site Design Group has cultivated its career on such fascinating projects, because the firm understands the universality of parks. ■ ■ ■ ■ ■ ■ ■ ■ ■ ■ ■

Peggy Notebaert Nature Museum

Perkins + Will

■ ■ ■ ■ ■ ■ ■ ■ ■ ■ For 150 years, the Chicago Academy of Sciences has been driven to bring the natural history of the Midwest to the present. In 1999 the Peggy Notebaert Nature Museum—an extension of the academy—fulfilled an innovative building mission. With the new build, the museum brought on Ralph Johnson of Perkins + Will. What Ralph brought was a grand scale image that revealed the bond that connects man with nature.

When the site was converted to a park in the 19th century, the conversion process cleared away the prevalent sand dunes that had a tendency to shift with the heavy winds. This geological incongruity returns to the museum, as Ralph designed the structure to exhibit angular masses that recall those shifting dunes. What this accomplishes is an aesthetic indeterminacy, a dynamic of the natural world that is typically lost in manmade structures. This sense of

FACING PAGE: Looking north, the museum clearly explores new design possibilities.
Project Design Team: Ralph Johnson, Tom Mozina and Jerry Johnson.
Photograph by James Steinkamp Photography

organics informs the bulk of the museum's design. The roof hovers just below the tree line, which gives the landscape smoothness and pays respect to the heights and volumes that nature has provided.

The building is implanted in the site, safeguarding existing trees and contours. The distinctive entry to this 73,000-square-foot project is an incision in the landscape, with a natural stone wall and stone paving. Beyond the lobby, a ravine with native planting connects the museum to the pond, revealing a continuous plane of geological visuals. The butterfly haven—a vast asylum for Midwest species—opens up to this pond, while views are maximized to reveal a correlation between the exhibits and the world outside. But the true marvel is the bird walk, a shrewd, raw-boned concoction that offers the woods unprocessed birding exhibits.

Ralph's design won a Distinguishing Building award from the Chicago chapter of the AIA, an American Architecture award from The Chicago Athenaeum and a Project of Distinction from the CEFPI. Taking a leap from contextual architecture into a new realm of metaphorical and biological building, Ralph and Perkins + Will have redefined showcasing, and the Peggy Notebaert Nature Museum propels Chicagoan design beyond its already elevated rank. ■ ■ ■ ■ ■ ■ ■ ■ ■ ■

ABOVE LEFT: The museum is designed never to superimpose the tree line.
Photograph by Nick Merrick, Hedrich Blessing Photography

ABOVE RIGHT: With a complex smoothness, the butterfly haven leads out to the birdwalk.
Photograph by Steinkamp/Ballogg Photography

FACING PAGE TOP LEFT: The outdoor dining terrace reveals the design, which mimics the historical sand dunes.
Photograph by Steinkamp/Ballogg Photography

FACING PAGE TOP RIGHT: The birdwalk is a great spot for budding ornithologists.
Photograph by Steinkamp/Ballogg Photography

FACING PAGE BOTTOM: A great preservation area, the museum is moments from downtown Chicago.
Photograph by Steinkamp/Ballogg Photography

Sullivan Center

Joseph Freed and Associates LLC

■ ■ ■ ■ ■ ■ ■ ■ ■ ■ Committed to long-term value and environmental sensitivity in all of its projects, Joseph Freed and Associates becomes a part of the neighborhood in which it has a development—constructing projects and then sticking around to run them effectively. Communities are built on their histories, and so the firm strives to adaptively reuse historically significant structures, including the fascinating downtown Chicago building complex Sullivan Center.

Chicago prides itself on its architecture and its homegrown architects like Louis Sullivan, the "father of modernism." Sullivan Center therefore offers a rare opportunity to create a 21st-century, mixed-use project that preserves the significant architectural elements of an iconic Sullivan creation.

FACING PAGE: The main entrance on State Street to the new office lobby reflects Louis Sullivan's mastery of cast-iron metalworking.
Photograph by Paul Schlismann

33
South State Street

CARSON PIRIE
SCOTT & CO.

CARSON PIRIE
SCOTT & CO.

Sullivan
Office Center

The historic preservation work alone is momentous. Starting with the upper-floor offices, Joseph Freed and Associates carefully restored and modernized the space to accommodate office, retail and dining uses. During the course of the redevelopment of these buildings, the team worked with the City of Chicago to restore the original Sullivan-designed cornices and cast iron on the exterior façade of the building—actually uncovering an unknown, original Sullivan cast iron in the process. In addition to restoring the exterior façades, interior spaces have been transformed into a mix of retail, entertainment and dining tenants to better serve the new neighborhood in this downtown area.

TOP LEFT: A newly restored office lobby welcomes workers and visitors to this landmark building.
Photograph by George Bartlett

BOTTOM LEFT: The dynamic lobby of the SAIC has creative projects on display.
Photograph by George Bartlett

FACING PAGE: One of the most recognizable historic structures in downtown Chicago, the building proudly displays its unique architectural details.
Photograph by Paul Schlismann

Nine separate buildings make up the complex, so the styles vary dramatically. The talents of Louis Sullivan and Daniel Burnham have been combined with the architectural styles of Wheelock & Thomas and John Mills Van Osdel to create Sullivan Center. Because of its central location in Chicago and the extensive Sullivan-designed architectural detailing on the exterior façades, Sullivan Center is perhaps Joseph Freed and Associates' most high-profile example of adaptive reuse—but the retail core and the sensitivity to the neighborhood influences the selection and variety of tenants in the project. Identifying the proper uses for the center and adapting a historic structure to those uses was challenging, but the firm's skills in finding the appropriate in long-term uses shines throughout Sullivan Center.

The balance of the space is being converted into class-A vintage office space—not only the home to the School of the Art Institute of Chicago but also the new headquarters for Joseph Freed and Associates. Winner of City of Chicago's 2006 Preservation of Excellence Award and the AIA's Divine Detail Award, Sullivan Center is a successful mixed-use development that represents adaptive reuse at its finest. ▪ ▪ ▪ ▪ ▪ ▪ ▪ ▪ ▪ ▪

Willow Creek Community Church

■ ■

Goss Pasma Blomquist Architects

■ ■ ■ ■ ■ ■ ■ ■ ■ Since the early 1970s Willow Creek Community Church has been shaping a new vision of church by using contemporary music, drama and *Bible* teaching. Located outside of Chicago, Willow Creek has watched the congregation grow to more than 20,000 people each weekend. In the late 1990s the church teamed with Douglas Pasma of Goss Pasma Blomquist Architects and developed a masterplan that provided for ministry growth and facility expansion for the next 20 years. The featured component of this plan is an auditorium structure housing a worship style that utilizes all of the theater and dramatic arts, high-energy contemporary music, creative multimedia, and relevant *Bible*-based teaching.

This is no ordinary church. There are no stained glass windows, pews, pipe organs or other elements traditionally associated with church. Upon entering, you travel through a light-filled, double-height lobby space fitted with grand stairways, escalators, information kiosks and a water wall in the center. Informal

FACING PAGE: The massive auditorium looks out to a wonderful rock garden.
Project Design Team: Douglas Pasma, Mark Blomquist, Richard Barrows, Dennis Garde, with Senior Pastor Bill Hybels and Scott Troeger.
Photograph by Steve Hall, Hedrich Blessing Photography

sitting areas and a café with a fireplace promote casual relational activity and send a clear message: Come to church and stay for a while. Proceeding into the auditorium, the room presents a proscenium stage flanked on each side by large expanses of window wall with views into a beautifully landscaped rock formation/water element. The seating area—with 7,095 theater seats—wraps intimately around the stage on three levels. A material palette of rock-faced stone, stained millwork paneling/trim and perforated metal provides a warm, comfortable yet progressive feel for a church that strives in every way to "meet people where they are" and to be a relevant ministry in their lives.

The inspiration and challenge was to create a building that would facilitate a multifaceted worship style. The Goss Pasma Blomquist team managed to create a malleable building, one that would evolve with the ministry and with the ever-changing face of Christian worship. Willow Creek Community Church, supported by its architecture, is a very lively, uplifting and engaging building—which is what a church should be. ■ ■ ■ ■ ■ ■ ■ ■ ■ ■ ■

TOP LEFT: A mix of building elements can be seen at the West Atrium lobby entrance.
Photograph by Kevin Beswick

BOTTOM LEFT: The children's area has a check-in desk for easy organization.
Photograph by Steve Hall, Hedrich Blessing Photography

FACING PAGE LEFT: The sun-shade canopy meets the rock garden.
Photograph by Kevin Beswick

FACING PAGE RIGHT: A grand staircase in the atrium blends nicely with a water curtain.
Photograph by Steve Hall, Hedrich Blessing Photography

Wrigley Building

■ ■

Powell/Kleinschmidt, Inc.
David Zeunert & Associates, Inc.

■ ■ ■ ■ ■ ■ ■ ■ ■ ■ In the 1920s Wrigley Building became the first architectural venture north of the Chicago River. Over the decades the building would see two problems: One, the railroad lines blew dirt over the light-colored terracotta exterior that required acid for cleaning, which, in turn, ate away at the surface; and two, the influx of modernity, such as ATMs, slowly overcrowded the lobby. In the 1980s the chewing gum magnates decided to renovate—not just the surface but the total infrastructure and lobby. The joint venture project went to Powell/Kleinschmidt and David Zeunert & Associates.

Over the years the Wrigley family has maintained ownership of the building. Because of their pride in the structure, it was important to honor the elements of the original base building architecture, while sustaining modern elements. Robert Kleinschmidt and David Zeunert took extra care in ensuring Wrigley

FACING PAGE: These are the original elevator doors with the geometric design cast in bronze. The renovation included custom carpet design for elevator cabs in Wrigley Spearmint Green and panels behind elevator door grills.
Photograph by Nick Merrick, Hedrich Blessing Photography

approval at each step. Finding the original drawings, the pair directed a refurbishment that is geared to Wrigley Building's historical majesty, including the restoration of the two-story entrance. Since all of the modern conveniences had been pushed into the lobby, a great clearing followed. Marbling was placed to match the exact dimensions of the opening of the rotunda—the architects even found themselves in Georgia hunting down the perfect light-colored marble with as little veining as possible.

Along with the new flooring and walls—together with the restitution of a large central column—the transformation incorporated a total reworking of Wrigley Building's mechanical systems, most remarkable of which are the elevators. The bronze grillwork is some of the richest in Chicago; maintaining the majesty of this iconic bronze design proved a judicious, architectural feat. At base level, Robert and David were able to subtly, and tastefully, bring in some of the Wrigley green into the elevator's carpeting.

TOP LEFT: The design concept consisted of bringing the lobby back to its original two-story height, allowing daylight penetration into the entire space.
Photograph by Nick Merrick, Hedrich Blessing Photography

BOTTOM LEFT: The original clocks were preserved as a recall of history and to create the sense of a rotunda in the elevator lobby.
Photograph by Nick Merrick, Hedrich Blessing Photography

FACING PAGE: The building was designed in 1921 by renowned Chicago architects Graham, Anderson, Probst & White. It was the first building after the Chicago fire built north of the Chicago River and started the renaissance of Michigan Avenue and the Magnificent Mile.
Photograph by Nick Merrick, Hedrich Blessing Photography

During the two years of work, the owner never wanted one day of inconvenience for his tenants—Robert and David never closed the Michigan Avenue entrance. This commitment to the business illustrates the sense of pride that the Wrigley family has for the building. And they could sense this same commitment in Robert and David, for the pair's similar tastes and ability to collaborate, in the end, flourished in the renovation of one of Chicago's most prominent structures. ■ ■ ■ ■ ■ ■ ■ ■ ■ ■

CHAPTER FOUR
Industry Leaders

Gone are the days of stark white, sterile-feeling health care buildings and unimaginative institutional establishments. First impressions are paramount, and architects are charged with creating the intangible "experience" before the actual experience even begins. Among these pages this magic is showcased in LCM Architects' Access Living, educational projects such as Johnson & Lee Architects/Planners and VOA Associates' Kennedy-King College and DeStefano and Partners' Walter Payton College Preparatory High School, and health care facilities including Stephen Rankin Associates' Marianjoy Rehabilitation Hospital.

These industry projects are as expansive as they are high profile, so the community is fittingly engaged, perhaps more so in these enterprises than in any other. The talented professionals who have created the featured buildings are very conscious of this fact; it is what drives them to exceed the high expectations set forth from inception.

Advocate Lutheran General Hospital Center for Advanced Care, OWP/P, page 220

McCormick Place Convention Center, TVS Design, page 204

University of Illinois at Chicago Student Recreation Facility, PSA-Dewberry, page 210

Access Living

■ ■

LCM Architects

■ ■ ■ ■ ■ ■ ■ ■ ■ When LCM Architects set out to design a new building for Access Living, universal and green concepts became the impetus for the design. Access Living is a nonprofit center for independent living, promoting the inclusion of people with disabilities in every aspect of community life. To reflect this mission, this building needed to be inclusive in every sense of the word. In addition, the building needed to address the needs of the staff, a large percentage of which has some form of disability.

Designing a building to meet the varying needs of people with disabilities led LCM to apply the seven principles of universal design. Under universal design, all people, disabled or not, are treated in a uniform, dignified manner, and these universal elements are transparent. The Chicago Avenue site was sold to Access Living by the City of Chicago, and as a prerequisite, the building had to be green. The marriage of these two elements provided an initial challenge to LCM, but as the design unfolded, there proved to be a strong synergy between the two design paradigms.

FACING PAGE: The lobby lounge of Access Living opens to Chicago Avenue.
Photograph by George Lambros, Lambros Photography, Inc.

The design started with the site. While close public transportation stops contributed to the building's LEED rating, the careful detailing of the entry drop-off sequence became the first hint of universal design. A heated sidewalk keeps clear and dry in the winter, and the automatic doors welcome all visitors without effort or the use of a push plate. A dark stripe in the sidewalk provides an entrance location queue and continues into the building, providing a visual link to the reception desk. Once inside the building, the overlapping goals of universal design and green design become even more apparent. LCM worked with a consultant, Sieben Energy Associates, to incorporate energy-efficient features, such as lighting sensors that balance natural and artificial light levels while providing a high quantity of light for people with visual impairments. The zoned HVAC system provides climate control for individuals who have difficulty regulating their body temperature.

LEFT: From Chicago Avenue, the front elevation reveals an interesting glass and brick façade.
Photograph by George Lambros, Lambros Photography, Inc.

FACING PAGE LEFT: The team areas were designed openly, for ease of use.
Photograph by George Lambros, Lambros Photography, Inc.

FACING PAGE RIGHT: The reception area needs little signage as a result of universal design.
Photograph by George Lambros, Lambros Photography, Inc.

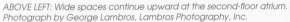

ABOVE LEFT: Wide spaces continue upward at the second-floor atrium. Photograph by George Lambros, Lambros Photography, Inc.

ABOVE RIGHT: One of the features of universal design is legless tables. Photograph by George Lambros, Lambros Photography, Inc.

However, what works for one disability does not always work for another, and that became apparent during the selection of floor material. When testing a carpet for easy wheelchair movement, the pattern in the carpet sample triggered a seizure for an employee. The solution became a carpet with a more muted overall pattern, accented with a contrasting border to help guide persons with visual impairments. In addition to the common elements, the workstations were also selected to be adjustable. Based on careful testing, Steelcase modified one of its standard file components for use at Access Living and later made it available as a standard component option.

Other items that may not be apparent but are key factors of universal design are the design of doorless public toilet rooms, pass-through elevators that assist in wheelchair circulation and varying sizes and types of furniture. To top it off, the green roof, with an outdoor terrace, not only helps with urban heat island mitigation and with reduction in stormwater runoff, but also presents an attractive view.

Being a good neighbor to the surrounding community was a high priority for Access Living. LCM designed a clean, simple, "quiet modern" building that pays respect to the local architecture, utilizing brick as a background material to harmonize with surrounding buildings, while accenting the street façade with plenty of glass.

After receiving a 2007 Chicago AIA Sustainable Design Award and the 2007 Paralyzed Veterans of America's Barrier-Free America Award, the building has generated interest from other architects and developers. The first question often asked is, "How much more did it cost?" Because virtually every product specified is commercially available, the premium was minimal.

This building is one of the first examples of commercial architecture that has successfully been able to merge the concepts of sustainability and universal design. Many would argue that this is the direction architecture is taking: healthier buildings that everyone can use. And that is certainly a step in the right direction. ■ ■ ■ ■ ■ ■ ■ ■ ■ ■ ■

Kennedy-King College

■ ■

Johnson & Lee Architects/Planners, Ltd.
VOA Associates, Incorporated

■ ■ ■ ■ ■ ■ ■ ■ ■ How does a community college increase its enrollment by more than 30 percent three semesters in a row and counting? Through clever planning, enticing programs and striking new architecture—not just any architecture, but rather a thoughtful collection of collegiate-like buildings that breaks down the barriers of the unknown and engages the community. The original Kennedy-King College needed more than a facelift, so Mayor Daley and Chancellor Wayne Watson opted to move the campus down the street to an underutilized part of Englewood that had several things going for it: close proximity to two major bus lines, a rapid transit stop, gracious mature-growth trees and quite a few old foundations that could be repurposed into concrete fill for the site. Johnson & Lee Architects/Planners teamed up with VOA Associates to form the temporary entity Kennedy-King Architects, LLC, because the keys to a successful project are communication and a single-minded vision. The official partnership ensured that creative minds from varying backgrounds would be able to closely and constantly collaborate to masterplan and design the new campus.

FACING PAGE: The new Kennedy-King College has six buildings, with several buildings framing a traditional collegiate quadrangle.
Project Design Team: Chris Lee, Paul Hanson, Kim Clawson, Brandon Lipman, Raynay Valles and Steve Siegle.
Photograph by Ballogg Photography

Rather than working with one simple mega-building, as is traditional with two-year colleges in Chicago, the architects created a true campus, replete with a quadrangle and clock tower. Kennedy-King College is comprised of six buildings—four of which anchor the campus's corners, three of which are connected by covered walkways—focused outwardly to invite the public to enjoy its relaxed scholastic ambience while passing through, sample the academic offerings or participate in civic events. The Halsted Street side of the campus is wide open, so students and faculty as well as businesspeople, kids and others who would not normally happen upon the college grounds contribute to the vibrant atmosphere as well as its safety.

Ordinary citizens' involvement with the college began long before the new campus was complete. Johnson & Lee has a rich history of architecturally bettering neglected neighborhoods. Extending to the people of Englewood the same level of satisfaction and ownership they feel with each of their projects, the architects chose local artisans and craftsmen to undertake construction of the campus—the palette of brick was chosen over cast concrete expressly because of the readily available workforce of brick masons. This not only bolstered local commerce, it also instilled in the people who physically created the buildings—and their families and friends—a reverence for the campus. Perhaps their progeny are responsible for the upsurge of eager students.

The variety of Kennedy-King College's academic programs—and valuable feedback from professors—drove the architectural design. All of the spaces were designed with flexibility in mind so that the college can easily keep pace with evolving information technology. Many of the spaces are multifunctional: The dining room is great for town hall meetings and the auditorium is perfect for filming demonstrations and lectures. From the student-run book and reprographics shops to an auto mechanics program that services some of the city's fleets and a daycare operated by early childhood development students—ideal for young parents hard at schoolwork—the campus is a haven for learning that offers myriad services to the community, heightening the significance of its architecture.

ABOVE LEFT: The dining hall of the culinary program is designed to be flexible.
Photograph by Ballogg Photography

ABOVE RIGHT: The stage in this 300-seat theater can facilitate a moveable kitchen, allowing for the recording of the culinary program's cooking demonstrations.
Photograph by Ballogg Photography

FACING PAGE LEFT: Just one of the many athletic features at the two-year college is the natatorium.
Photograph by Ballogg Photography

FACING PAGE RIGHT: The high-tech, stainless steel kitchen embodies the culinary program.
Photograph by Ballogg Photography

Kennedy-King College is infused with earth-friendly elements: low-E windows with sun baffles, green roofs and exterior light fixtures that minimize light pollution. But the architects maintain that sustainability goes far beyond just being green. Their plan has ensured constant use of the buildings, and the design has quite literally been a sustaining, rejuvenating force for the community, spurring retail development, affordable housing projects and new fire and police stations. Architect Chris Lee, FAIA, grew up in Englewood, so the chance to participate in the community's renaissance was particularly meaningful to him. Yet the whole design team, the people who built it, the people who interact with it and the neighbors who live by it all take pride in the creation of Kennedy-King College, a magnetic public park of knowledge. ■ ■ ■ ■ ■ ■ ■ ■ ■ ■

RIGHT: The entrance into the academic building is warm and inviting with its brick and open glass façade.
Photograph by Ballogg Photography

FACING PAGE LEFT: Natural daylighting blankets the student commons.
Photograph by Ballogg Photography

FACING PAGE RIGHT: The athletic corridor shows the subtle brick pattern that lightens at the second floor.
Photograph by Ballogg Photography

McCormick Place Convention Center

TVS Design

■ ■ ■ ■ ■ ■ ■ ■ ■ Flames engulfed McCormick Place in 1967, burning down what was thought to be an indestructible building. Now, McCormick

Place is the largest convention center in the United States, a complex with a scale that reaches unfathomable depths. With some three million visitors

a year, McCormick Place is a four-building, state-of-the-art venue that stretches across nearly three million square feet of event space. Owned and

managed by the Metropolitan Pier and Exposition Authority, McCormick Place has gone through major expansions, including the most recent McCormick

Place West. Involved in the conceptual and design stages since 1990, TVS Design has taken McCormick Place West into remarkable new territories.

ABOVE: The east elevation—the formal edge—of the West Expansion and the conference center are viewed from McCormick Square Plaza.
Photograph by James Steinkamp Photography, courtesy of Epstein

FACING PAGE: A cantilever lantern at the civic edge identifies the primary entrance to the West Expansion.
Project Design Team: Tom Ventulett, Mike Hagen, Andrew McLean, Jay Thomson and Mike Azumi.
Photograph by James Steinkamp Photography, courtesy of Epstein

Although leviathan in scale, McCormick Place West is designed to function at the human level. Part of this process involves the expression toward four distinct faces of Chicago. With freeways, civic spaces, a neighborhood and the highway, the design seeks to meet the elements halfway. The neighborhood edge, for example, elevates with brick and other small works to reflect the residential-scale aesthetics. This exterior seeks to respect, preserve and enhance the surrounding area while encouraging new development in other areas. The building never turns its back to the neighborhoods; façades of glass and plenty of light make it approachable, transparent and welcoming. A 90-foot lantern, with glass on three sides, cantilevers out from the face of the building and creates a canopy over the west entrance, in a unique and beautiful architectural element.

But of course the scale is awe-inspiring. The West building boasts one of the largest ballrooms in the world, at 100,000 square feet—Soldier Field could sit comfortably inside. The ballroom can be configured in 15 different fashions, with theater-style seating available for 11,000 people. With 470,000 square feet of exhibition space and 250,000 square feet of meeting space over 61 meeting rooms, McCormick Place West offers a huge range of flexibility in event possibilities. Even the rooftop garden can host an event of up to 800 people, a great pre-function space for Chicago's famous views.

One of the amazing feats for McCormick Place West was its achievement of LEED certification. Finding daylighting for a building of this magnitude is a large accomplishment—achieved in part through open-glassed, multilevel spaces. TVS Design even cut out the middleman with its stormwater collection; rather than designing a typical system, the firm tunneled to Lake Michigan, sending stormwater back to the lake.

RIGHT: From inside, the lantern looks out west.
Photograph by James Steinkamp Photography, courtesy of Epstein

FACING PAGE TOP LEFT: Concourses are large multilevel people spaces that serve as the public circulation spines within the complex.
Photograph by James Steinkamp Photography, courtesy of Epstein

FACING PAGE TOP RIGHT: The cantilever lantern identifies the primary entrance.
Photograph by James Steinkamp Photography, courtesy of Epstein

FACING PAGE BOTTOM: The Skyline Ballroom also serves to accommodate exhibits.
Photograph by James Steinkamp Photography, courtesy of Epstein

McCormick Place West is transforming its neighborhood. Showcasing 30 commissioned art pieces by Chicago and Illinois artists, McCormick Place West is local sentiments on a grand scale. MPEA's desire to keep Chicago competitive has not only created one of the largest and most interesting event spaces in the world but is also propelling the job force. At the opening ceremony, a plaque was unveiled that listed the names of the crew who worked on and at the McCormick Place site. There were some 6,000 names.

ABOVE: The curved bridge connects the Wet Expansion Central Concourse with the South Expansion Grand Concourse.
Photograph by James Steinkamp Photography, courtesy of Epstein

FACING PAGE: A ground-level setback serves as the limousine and valet parking drop-off. The Skyline Ballroom pre-function space is located behind the large expanse of curtainwall. Directly below the roof overhang is an outdoor garden.
Photograph by James Steinkamp Photography, courtesy of Epstein

University of Illinois at Chicago
Student Recreation Facility

■ ■

PSA-Dewberry

■ ■ ■ ■ ■ ■ ■ ■ ■ Educating some 20,000 students a year, the University of Illinois at Chicago had always been a commuter college due to its location in the heart of Chicago. The social element for the school was falling a bit flat, despite having the nation's largest medical school. On campuses, recreation centers have a tendency to draw students in, a veritable YMCA between classes. Since the existing recreation center had little drawing power, UIC sought a new facility that would relate to the campus while building student life by being different than the norm. UIC commissioned PSA-Dewberry—a specialist in medical wellness and recreation centers—to develop a unique architectural program, one that reflected both the city of Chicago and the UIC campus, as well as one that carried a premise of movement, parallel to the agile actions of the human body.

FACING PAGE: The aerial view of the UIC recreation center roots the facility in its place along the eastern edge of the campus, with the city in the background. During the evening the facility glows, allowing students to view the activity within.
Project Design Team: Christopher Frye and Tom Seymour.
Photograph by Ballogg Photography

Sited on the northeast corner of UIC, the Student Recreation Facility is a gateway building, sitting at the edge of city and campus. In this manner, PSA-Dewberry's design called for components that were relatable to the other buildings on campus as well as the aesthetics of the metropolis. Rather than an enclosed box, a very open structure was created. Using lots of glass reveals the life inside, so passersby see the bustling activity. Like those of the athletes, the velocities of the building adjust depending on pedestrian activity. One direction is articulated for transparency, while another side slows the eye, elongating the ambler's experience.

Often, an athlete's greatest asset is the skin—calluses can be a determining factor in performance. With a largely metal-skinned façade, the SRF uses the building's skin to enhance aesthetically the athleticism inside. Metal surfaces peel back to reveal glass openings, while precast concrete cuts through to make way for metal and warming terracotta-hued sections, all in a great layering of the tactile experience.

The central organizing mechanism is an internal courtyard woven into the center. Designed for movement, all major spaces vertically or horizontally extend from here. The three-story central atrium now functions almost as a student center in its own right.

TOP RIGHT: The natatorium is an exploration in movement, folding down toward the water within and bending back upward to address the greater campus fabric. It anchors the corner of the site giving gesture back to the student union across the street. Photograph by Ballogg Photography

BOTTOM RIGHT: Transparency becomes as much a material as a quality. Views from afar announce the various activities within. Drought-resistant natural plantings are used around the facility. The original trees that surround the site were maintained, demonstrating the university's commitment to the stewardship of the environment. Photograph by Ballogg Photography

FACING PAGE: From the exterior one can read the facility, allowing view deep within. The entry plaza is framed by the three-story atrium glass, with the folded roof of the natatorium providing visual direction to the front door. Photograph by Ballogg Photography

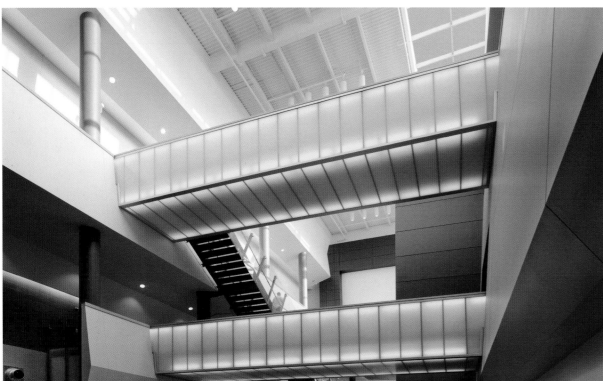

But it is here, upon entry, that visitors become aware of the layering components of the center; major sections seem shifted in their spaces, so that overlapping is apparent and understandable. Like the body, the flesh and bones of the building are in continuous activity, bending and stretching, working against the force of the other.

To heighten the sense of spatial dynamic, the functions of the SRF stack atop one another over the three levels. This high-tech facility has not only the common functions, such as gymnasiums and exercise equipment rooms and indoor pools but also, for those harsh Chicago winters, an indoor jogging track and courts for badminton and soccer, and a 50-person Jacuzzi. As well, a three-story rock-climbing wall shoots up 45 feet, while a juice and coffee bar sits just beyond for those after-workout, social moments—or to enjoy a beverage while watching someone repel down three stories.

A great first step in the UIC campus, the SRF serves as an effective recruitment tool for the university. Through this nearly anthropomorphic building, PSA-Dewberry has created a fascinating addition to the UIC campus and has reinterpreted the possibilities in recreational complexes. ■ ■ ■ ■ ■ ■ ■ ■ ■ ■

TOP LEFT: At the main entry, the racquetball volume hovers precariously overhead, while beyond the main communicating stair climbs up three stories.
Photograph by Ballogg Photography

TOP RIGHT: From the third-floor fitness floor, one can view the inside-outside relationship of the various volumes while allowing students views into the natatorium below.
Photograph by Ballogg Photography

BOTTOM LEFT: Two lighted bridges cross the 70-plus-foot atrium give a heightened sense of space within this interior courtyard. With the ample natural light one has the feeling of being outside.
Photograph by Ballogg Photography

FACING PAGE: The natatorium contains a large leisure component as well as the traditional lap pool. The folded roof is supported by the large trusses that come within seven-and-a-half feet of the water, giving a strong sense of compression, as opposed to the sense of uplift given by the lobby.
Photograph by Ballogg Photography

1363 Shermer

Myefski Cook Architects

■ ■ ■ ■ ■ ■ ■ ■ ■ ■ On many main streets across America, maintaining character while promoting vitality is a delicate balance. The village of Northbrook, Illinois, is no exception, where residents and village officials alike have a renewed interest in strengthening activity in their central business district to complement the village's outlying office, shopping and dining districts. When the idea to redevelop a high-profile site in the village center came about, one very distinct element had to be carefully considered: How can a structure be the first of its kind and not be remarkably out of place? The developer of 1363 Shermer approached Myefski Cook Architects with a rare opportunity to create something unique for Northbrook, under the watchful eyes of this proud village.

The triangular site for this office building is directly adjacent to train tracks, a 25-minute ride from Chicago's own bustling downtown. This location next to a commuter rail station suited the building's proposed use perfectly: provide both a professional working environment close to home and a meeting space for

those traveling to and from work in Chicago. After working with village officials, the commuter rail company and local utilities for two years, approval was in hand and construction was underway.

Breaking with traditional organization of office spaces, the unique triangular geometry of 1363 Shermer paralleled the developer's intent to provide a unique working environment as part of his shared office

concept. The structure also reflects unique site characteristics—its poured-in-place concrete walls and floors assist in minimizing vibration, while laminated glass reduces noise from the active train schedule visible just outside any east window. The offices are enclosed with a taut masonry façade with a regular rhythm of alternating punch openings and boxed bay windows. Each of these three faces terminates in cylindrical corners, which mimics spools of thread. Subtle changes in brick color are also utilized, with the narrower southern façade clad in white limestone, reflecting summer heat. The hint of historic detailing at the corner towers grounds the building, topped with metal cornices that also shield the building's mechanical systems.

At three stories, the building has greater presence than seen in surrounding structures, but it meets the street at a human scale to which all can relate. Recessed glass openings and canopies engage pedestrians seeking shelter on their way to catch the next train, or headed to the diner currently planned at the northern, first-floor corner space. At the center canopy, the building's main entry, tenants and visitors alike are greeted by a concierge stationed within the lobby.

Myefski Cook Architects selected interior finishes, planning for furniture and dramatic locations for artwork, for the first-floor lobby as well as for the offices on floors two and three. In addition to private offices, there are also shared conference facilities, a clubroom with pool table, kitchenettes and support spaces on those levels.

With its proximity to public transportation and work environments close to home, 1363 Shermer is the new dynamic of sustainable building, where contemporary needs, technology and aesthetics find harmony in a main street setting. With 1363 Shermer, Myefski Cook Architects has succeeded in elevating a community—a great statement for Northbrook's progress and for architectural openness.

RIGHT: Subtle brick and limestone variations, combined with the rhythm of various fenestration elements and cantilevered canopies along the street front, enliven this stretch of Northbrook's downtown district.
Photograph by Tony Soluri Photography

FACING PAGE LEFT: Dynamic, functional design elements on the exterior both engage and intrigue, from strategically placed street-level canopies to the radiused mechanical screens that emulate traditional metal cornices.
Photograph by Tony Soluri Photography

FACING PAGE RIGHT: A ribbed, curved, wood-veneered wall draws visitors into the richly appointed lobby and concierge area.
Photograph by Tony Soluri Photography

Advocate Lutheran General Hospital
Center for Advanced Care

■ ■

OWP/P

■ ■ ■ ■ ■ ■ ■ ■ ■ ■ Fifty years ago a trip to the hospital offered few things: white walls, crowded halls and doctors who prescribed remedies as if they were reading off a recipe card. Thankfully, the days of opaque doctor-patient relationships are a thing of the past, but health care buildings have not immediately followed this paradigm. Creating such large-scale projects requires the talent and creativity of dozens of architects, engineers, interior designers and tradespeople. The professionals of OWP/P were met with an outdated building among many other challenges when Advocate Lutheran General Hospital needed to move outpatient imaging to a lower level of the facility. Such a revitalization provided an opportunity to expand key services and create a cancer center that could further the hospital's mission while providing patients with an even more satisfactory experience.

FACING PAGE: The center has an inviting presence. Its transparency highlights the warm, simple interiors.
Design Team Members: Gregory A. Heiser, Randy Guillot, Troy Hoggard, Aaron Shepard and Dennis Ryan.
Photograph by James Steinkamp

After assessing the hospital campus, it became clear to the design team that constructing a new facility was not an option. Space constraints—and recently purchased accelerator vaults—guided the team to renovate and add 54,500 square feet to the West Pavilion, an older building designed during the 1960s' "Hill-Burton" era. While the existing structure might not have been accurately described as "gloomy," it was certainly not in step with modern medicine. With limited natural light, poor air circulation, floor-to-floor heights of just 10 feet—four to five feet less than today's standards—and its bland, nondescript ambience, the existing architecture presented the design team with a large task.

Overall, the space reflected an outdated model of care and renovations called for removing the entire front of the building. To create a dramatic image and make the building visible from the main campus road, a distinctive leading edge, or "prow," was incorporated by stretching the addition's envelope. It houses the three-story atrium, which acts as the circulation spine connecting the Cancer Care Center, Center for Advanced Imaging and Caldwell Breast Center; not only does it flood the space with sunlight, but it aids wayfinding while protecting patient privacy with three separate campus entrances. Overlapping elements and design horizontality soothed any tension and brought cohesion to the three separate entities.

Interior spaces were reprogrammed to create a patient-friendly environment, address staff needs and improve operational efficiencies by clustering services. Inspired by the native prairies of the Midwest, the Center for Advanced Care is no longer an uninviting stark envelope, but rather its spring hues are fresh and encourage optimism. Patterned glass provides privacy while the geometry and materials allow natural light to interact and penetrate clinical areas. Taking into account the continuity of finishes and nature-inspired materials for a cohesive image, the design embraces and nurtures patients, their families and staff.

Logical and intuitive, the center's architectural design has helped the hospital achieve its vision of providing a multidisciplinary destination that offers advanced imaging and health services—outpatient services have been consolidated in this warm and comfortable state-of-the-art facility. Its clinic module, room sizes and department layouts offer the hospital a valuable flexibility to adapt to changing care models, technology and programmatic needs. A catalyst for change, the renovation of the Center for Advanced Care has not only redefined the hospital's image, but has set the tone for future development and a new branding for the Chicago campus. ■ ■ ■ ■ ■ ■ ■ ■ ■ ■

TOP RIGHT: The building creates a strong edge to the campus, reflecting the context around it.
Photograph by James Steinkamp Photography

BOTTOM RIGHT: The project's interior spaces are flooded with diffused natural light. The palette of the interior reflects the themes of optimism, transparency and quality care.
Photograph by James Steinkamp Photography

FACING PAGE TOP LEFT: The building's prow announces the cancer program's presence in an elegant and distinctive way.
Photograph by James Steinkamp Photography

FACING PAGE TOP RIGHT: The first-floor resource center is a relaxing and informative element at the heart of the building.
Photograph by Steve Hall, Hedrich Blessing Photography

FACING PAGE BOTTOM: The entrance to the imaging department is open and inviting. A large glass wall overlooks a garden space, offering a natural complement to the center's interior palette.
Photograph by James Steinkamp Photography

Marianjoy Rehabilitation Hospital

■ ■

Stephen Rankin Associates

■ ■ ■ ■ ■ ■ ■ ■ ■ A distinct paradox exists in rehabilitation hospitals: Patients have average stays of almost 20 days, but are not really sick. The new replacement Marianjoy Rehabilitation Hospital is a transition point through the continuum of care. When Stephen Rankin Associates was first commissioned to build this new hospital, Stephen traveled with Kathleen Yosko, the president and CEO of Marianjoy, to several other facilities to observe patients movement. These studies became the genesis of a new approach to design for rehabilitative care.

There are few less helpful metaphors in a hospital than being encumbered and met by dead ends. Stephen Rankin Associates began its design by freeing up circulation. Through careful positioning, Marianjoy has eliminated dead-end conditions, ensuring smooth and continual traffic flow. Whether pushed via wheelchair or utilizing walkers, patients at all times have wider berths of passage and circular movement through looped hallways. Even the

FACING PAGE: Marianjoy's new shape can be seen at the main entry pavilion and patient drop-off.
Project Design Team: Stephen Rankin, Brian Hirami, Takemasa Okugawa and Linda Chin.
Photograph by Christopher Barrett, Hedrich Blessing Photography

therapy gyms and patient treatment rooms, where possible, have two ways to enter. Moreover, by bifurcating the entire three-story building, the design team opened up a courtyard that centralizes the movement and allows patients and staff to successfully orient themselves within the hospital. Undulation of the building edges means there are no disheartening views down infinite hallways. Windows are positioned so that patients can enjoy views from their beds, thereby reducing neck strain.

In order to save the maximum numbers of climax oak and hickory trees on the Wheaton Franciscan Sisters' campus, the new Marianjoy building was restricted to a four-acre plot of land that was formerly a surface parking lot.

The main axis of the hospital, with an entry pavilion, an enabling garden and a new chapel, radiates from a central, circular courtyard. Through collaboration with the hospital, a labyrinth was developed within the circle, identical in scale and shape to the labyrinth in the nave of Chartres Cathedral in France. Around this labyrinth is a below-grade connection to the old building and to the new parking structure, which is positioned to allow copious amounts of daylight to shine on the patients or visitors as they gather in the space. Grade changes were minimized, and the new four-level parking deck is handicap accessible throughout.

Design with a keen sensitivity to disability issues is of paramount importance in a rehabilitation facility. Patients' understanding and ease of mobility in navigation of the space must be immediate. To accommodate single private rooms and ADA requirements Marianjoy tripled the square-footage of the patient areas from that in the old hospital while retaining the same number of patient beds. By taking into consideration the needs of the residents, as well as the staff, Stephen Rankin Associates has developed a fascinating prototype that brings flow of movement, light, safety and serenity to rehabilitation design. The saying in rehab medicine, that we are all only temporarily able-bodied, is a characterization that Rankin took to heart in designing the Marianjoy Rehabilitation Hospital. The end result is a successful design with universal appeal. ■ ■ ■ ■ ■ ■ ■ ■ ■ ■

ABOVE LEFT: The new chapel faces a Shagbark Hickory that is slightly offset from the cross.
Photograph by Christopher Barrett, Hedrich Blessing Photography

BOTTOM LEFT: Glass walls open up the entry stair and elevator tower to the new parking deck.
Photograph by Christopher Barrett, Hedrich Blessing Photography

BOTTOM RIGHT: The south building elevation co-exists with the existing climax oak trees.
Photograph by Christopher Barrett, Hedrich Blessing Photography

ABOVE: The articulated chapel wall has colored stained glass and a fully aproned glass railing at the patient balcony.
Photograph by Christopher Barrett, Hedrich Blessing Photography

FACING PAGE: A labyrinth garden fronts an all-weather pedestrian connector and vehicular drop-off at the main entry.
Photograph by Christopher Barrett, Hedrich Blessing Photography

Naperville Public Library
95th Street Facility

■ ■

PSA-Dewberry

■ ■ ■ ■ ■ ■ ■ ■ ■ ■ Naperville, Illinois, is a booming city. Voted one of the top places to live in the United States, Naperville blossomed under the influx of many professionals. As the town grew outward, Naperville Public Library sought to expand its branches with a third and largest branch on 95th Street, a main drag with high exposure on the south end of Naperville. Trying to capture both the historical relevance of the site, as well as the civic image of an outwardly expanding city, NPL acquired PSA-Dewberry for the project. Christopher Frye, AIA, created with this 95th Street NPL Facility a library that affords public access to the latest technology and makes an architectural statement on both civic-building and historical-reference possibilities.

FACING PAGE: The two-story lobby visually connects all the departments of the library, anchored by the monumental stair wrapping around the terracotta-clad elevator shaft. The area is further heightened by the monitor directly above.
Project Design Team: Christopher Frye and Randy Gibson.
Photograph by Ballogg Photography

Everyone knew of the farms that sat on this agrarian landscape. Part of the design was to develop a barn-like aesthetic to the building's façade. The library is divided into three sections: a main collection of child and adult materials, a popular materials section, and an information commons and administration offices. These separate sections are shifted to conform to an irregular site—one that curves and drops. Recalling the vernacular of the old barns, these three building forms are overarched by a large roof plate that bends to function as an organizing element.

The library's board of directors was looking for a "high-tech, high-touch" aesthetic—something advanced in technology but also inviting and approachable to visitors. Much of this feel was achieved through the use of terracotta as the primary building material. Large expanses of glass allow a clean transition of visuals from indoors to outdoors and vice versa. Since the library sits on 95th Street, it was important for vehicular traffic to notice life inside this building. As well, in the division of the two levels of floor space, a visual connection spreads out between the floors, creating an open volume that would be lost in a sectional building.

NPL really wanted the 95th Street branch to be differentiated from the other two branches, and so the group was willing to take risks that proved worth the effort; in fact, the library use doubled its anticipated numbers.

Rather than trying to match the traditional imagery of public spaces, NPL shaped this building to reflect a new community with a lot of soul. With no preconceived notions about what a civic building should be, PSA-Dewberry created a building that redefines library spaces. Because of this interest in cutting-edge didacticism, Naperville Public Library was the top-rated library system from 1999 to 2006 by the American Library Association. ■ ■ ■ ■ ■ ■ ■ ■ ■ ■

Second Federal Savings

■ ■

W. Steven Gross / Architectural Associates

■ ■ ■ ■ ■ ■ ■ ■ ■ ■ One of the great things about Chicago is its diversity. Little pockets of varying ethnicities have a tendency to break up the banal paradigm. The Brighton Park neighborhood, in southwest Chicago, was initially settled by European Jews and was soon followed by Polish immigrants. However, with the influx of Mexican immigration into the United States in the late '80s and '90s, Brighton Park became predominantly a Mexican community by the year 2000. One bank would take the first step in catering to this neighborhood's new majority.

Steven Gross came to Second Federal Savings under interesting circumstances. An old friend of his had become the president of the bank and asked him to design an addition to the bank's flagship office. Shortly after, he was asked to sit on the bank's board of directors and assist them in expanding into other similar Mexican neighborhoods in the Chicago metropolitan area. Because Second Federal is a Mutual, and owned by its depositors, it tends to

FACING PAGE: As a retail building, color, lighting and form were emphasized and highlighted to attract the passing motorists both night and day. Photograph by Steinkamp/Ballogg Photography

SECOND FEDERAL SAVINGS
SECOND
FEDERAL
CASH STATION
SECOND
FEDERAL
SAVINGS
SECOND
FEDERAL
SAVINGS

reinvest money back into the community, sometimes in the form of better-quality buildings. The resulting branch would be an interesting study in both ethnic allure and controversial building.

Site-wise, Second Federal Savings sits on one of the few angled streets on the big grid that is Chicago. The triangular building is an adaptive reuse of an existing, century-old building. Because of the drab, dismal, brick-and-stone neighborhood, Steven's design called for an explosion—of not only color, but of an Art Deco-like façade with unrivaled individuality. The Mexican culture tends toward brighter colors, and Second Federal Savings reflects that. Lilac blue and safety yellow make a definitive, colorful statement against the common color schemes. The theme continues inside, yet is muted to pastels.

TOP LEFT: The wedge-like site presented formal opportunities of composition that were exploited and stand in contrast to the usual grid-inspired façades lining the urban way.
Photograph by Steinkamp/Ballogg Photography

BOTTOM LEFT: Sky-like colors are reintroduced in the lobby, giving a serenity to the interior space.
Photograph by Steinkamp/Ballogg Photography

New forms were brought in for the branch, namely to contrast with the hard angles of the cityscape. Exterior scaffolding is exposed—a skeleton to enhance lighting and signage that simultaneously serves to screen HVAC units. The high-tech, curved signage and canopy panels change the façade according to the direction of approach. Though Steven and his team incorporated the basics of the existing building, this "new millennium" approach brings to a neighborhood in transition a successful local landmark.

Not often are architects offered the level of creative freedom that Steven was allowed on this project; nor, for that matter, are they asked to sit on the board of directors. The success of Second Federal Savings offers another example of how good design equates to good business. Second Federal Savings now has five branches—all of which are designed for the ethnic communities they serve, with each offering an unusual and exciting design opportunity for Steven.

RIGHT: An attention to detail is communicated in the awnings, signage and screening structure that attempt to convey a feeling of hi-tech/human-scaled craftsmanship. Photograph by Steinkamp/Ballogg Photography

United Auto Workers Region 4 Headquarters

■ ■

The Hezner Corporation

■ ■ ■ ■ ■ ■ ■ ■ ■ Ideological concepts associated with union affiliation traditionally have included those of organization, solidarity and strength. When the opportunity arose for a new headquarters for United Auto Workers Region 4 in Lincolnshire, Illinois, the UAW Region 4 director wanted to project these ideals into images and create a forward-thinking, sophisticated facility that is functional and comfortable, artistic, and interactive with the surrounding environment without being mundane or pretentious.

The Hezner Corporation and Hezcorp Construction Services designed and constructed the new headquarters over a 15-month period by applying a methodical design approach, an inherent knowledge of local municipal government, and by utilizing an experienced construction team well versed in

FACING PAGE: The main entrance to the headquarters shows the impressive stone division.
Project Design Team: Kurt E. Hezner, Scott K. Hezner, Patricia J. Green, Andrew Shimanski and Keith Schodin.
Photograph by Howard Kaplan, HNK Architectural Photographer, Inc

complex construction processes. The client had basic design and construction requirements: the architect must provide American-made and union-manufactured materials and systems, and the contractor had to assure that all labor and equipment used on the project would have union affiliation. The UAW Region 4 goal was to maintain a deliberate and literal domestic element as the basis for the project, which created the collaborative approach that is true to the mission and beliefs of the UAW. The result reflects a clear adherence and execution of this goal.

The building itself sits on five acres and is positioned on the southeast corner of the site, in close proximity to intersecting streets. Through the application of stone massing and crisp edge delineation, the outward architectural imagery reflects upon the UAW principles of strength and a straightforward approach to business. The elevations that face the adjacent streets have the most direct public exposure and, therefore, were to represent a fortified organization and solidarity. The elevations oriented toward the interior portions of the site are composed predominantly of glass curtainwall systems. These glazing arrangements create a literal and open connection with the natural beauty of the site, which represents the open and inclusive relationship that the UAW has with its membership. Linking the divergent architectural applications of stone

TOP LEFT: Careful design of the director's office ensured openness for the organization.
Photograph by Howard Kaplan, HNK Architectural Photographer, Inc

BOTTOM LEFT: Openness continues with welcoming offices.
Photograph by Howard Kaplan, HNK Architectural Photographer, Inc

FACING PAGE TOP: The east elevation shows the distinct elements of glass and rock.
Photograph by Howard Kaplan, HNK Architectural Photographer, Inc

FACING PAGE BOTTOM: From the north, the prominent façade conveys strength.
Photograph by Howard Kaplan, HNK Architectural Photographer, Inc

and glass is a large penetrating stone plane that symbolically connects and exemplifies the sustaining vitality and compassion that the UAW offers each member in the organization. The director wanted something different and meaningful, and this vision is represented in the completed building.

Clients who seek something different look for compelling reasons and solutions with substance. The UAW Region 4 felt that The Hezner Corporation inherently understood what they were looking for and liked the hands-on and vested approach the team brought to problem solving. The result is a beautifully composed building that serves the client's interests while being respectful to the community and the region where it is located. ■ ■ ■ ■ ■ ■ ■ ■ ■ ■

Walter Payton College Preparatory High School

DeStefano and Partners

■ ■ ■ ■ ■ ■ ■ ■ ■ ■ Since 1996 Chicago Public Schools has invested billions of dollars in its first major new construction and renovation program in decades. This ongoing effort is one element in the city's plan to revitalize its diverse neighborhoods by improving and enhancing urban infrastructure and public buildings. The expectation is that an improved school system will not only remedy years of neglect, but also will help retain and attract residents who contribute to the city's economic vitality.

DeStefano and Partners worked with CPS to develop a unique Managing Architect System that delivered more than 50 new schools and additions on schedule and on budget within an exceptionally compact four-year time frame. As a result of this highly effective approach, Chicago has been hailed as a model for its aggressive commitment to educational reform and commitment to urban viability.

FACING PAGE: The front entry is between two building "blocks," housing academic and support functions, linked by an enclosed circulation spine.
Project Design Team: James R. DeStefano and Mary Ann Van Hook.
Photograph by Barbara Karant, Karant + Associates, Inc.

As a result, Chicago can boast its first new public high schools in more than 20 years. To ensure educational opportunity for its diverse youth population, CPS is steadily investing in a district-wide system of high schools to provide a competitive college preparatory curriculum for high-achieving students. Walter Payton College Prep, today one of Illinois' top achievers by any testing scale, was among the first new selective enrollment high schools to open its doors in 2000.

The challenge for Payton was twofold: to create a technology-based environment that supports a curriculum of lab-centered learning and interactive/interdisciplinary problem solving; and to design,

on a fixed budget, a high school campus on a nontraditional, compact four-acre site. The solution is a completely technology "wired" school community of two separate building blocks with distinct functions—academic and support—that are linked by an enclosed circulation spine or internal "street." This secure atrium is an interactive space throughout the school day and accommodates public functions after hours.

Raised computer flooring with under-floor wiring brings computer access to every student, a first for the district. The school's high-tech ideals are reflected in the architectural details—colorful metal staircases in the four-story atrium, exposed steel trusses and terrazzo flooring in a colorful sound-wave pattern. Low-maintenance, long-life building materials and state-of-the-art mechanical/electrical systems promote cost efficiency and an environmentally friendly focus.

Most of the 21 classrooms, laboratories and a greenhouse conservatory are housed in the south wing, where natural light abounds. In the north wing are support facilities, including a large recital hall, practice gymnasium with locker rooms, cafeteria/full kitchen, resource center and administrative spaces. Light brick softens the building's mass to harmonize with the neighborhood's low-rise residential stock.

A microcosm of the city itself, Walter Payton College Prep is a highly successfully community where 800 students and supportive faculty thrive on the cultural diversity of urban living. Located within sight of the iconic Sears Tower and connected by technology to a world of learning far beyond its walls, the school provides an ideal environment to achieve its mission: nurturing leaders.

RIGHT: Payton Preparatory is an urban campus just a short ride away from the heart of downtown Chicago.
Photograph by Barbara Karant, Karant + Associates, Inc.

FACING PAGE LEFT: Colorful stairwells in the central atrium, or internal "street," are open to encourage social interaction and promote security.
Photograph by Barbara Karant, Karant + Associates, Inc.

FACING PAGE RIGHT: A lecture/recital hall is in the north wing with other "public" spaces.
Photograph by Barbara Karant, Karant + Associates, Inc.

CHAPTER FIVE
Sustaining Growth

The Great Law of The Iroquois Confederacy suggests that in our every deliberation, we must consider the impact of our decisions on the next seven generations.

The efforts of building design aimed at ensuring a more positive outlook for the future are evident in projects from Burnidge Cassell Associates' Harm A. Weber Academic Center to Yas Architecture's Vernon Hills Village Hall. The tenets, ideas and revelations of sustainability are nothing new: Our planet is affected by the way we live. However, the commitment to green building practices has grown and evolved into tangible methods, which architects are increasingly incorporating into their projects. From renewable materials to energy-conserving electrical resources—these architects are discovering new innovations that are changing architecture's impact on our world. It is a passionate topic, but this passion for discovering and incorporating renewable resources has brought green design and building to the forefront.

That these practices will soon become commonplace in all forms of construction is the hope of many architects. Beneficial techniques that were once thought impossible are now not only possible but affordable as well. The professionals who employ these commendable methods are eloquently lighting the way for others to follow.

Tuthill Corporate Headquarters, Serena Sturm Architects, Ltd., page 266

Vernon Hills Village Hall, Yas Architecture, LLC, page 270

340 on the Park, Solomon Cordwell Buenz, page 250

111 South Wacker

■ ■

Goettsch Partners

■ ■ ■ ■ ■ ■ ■ ■ ■ A welcome addition to Chicago's majestic skyline, 111 South Wacker is both an architectural and environmental achievement. Fittingly, the site on which it stands was originally the headquarters of USG, a building materials manufacturer, and part of the structure was preserved for the new 53-story tower, reducing construction expenditures and keeping material waste to a minimum. Though the project garnered significant media attention and a healthy variety of awards, the greatest upshot of the 1,457,000-square-foot building has been that it has raised awareness of the power of sustainable design.

FACING PAGE: The building's unique steel frame system widens at the base, providing a remarkably open space at the ground level.
Project Design Team: James Goettsch, Steven M. Nilles, Lawrence C. Weldon, Joseph Cliggott, Aaron Greven, Joseph Schultz and Scott Seyer.
Photograph by James Steinkamp Photography

The landmark 111 South Wacker building came to fruition as a collaborative venture between two locally based organizations—The John Buck Company, a forward-thinking developer, and Goettsch Partners, an internationally respected architecture firm with roots tracing to Mies van der Rohe's practice. With the foundation of a successful previous project together, the duo had full confidence that this building would be another striking addition to the city.

Located in the heart of downtown—close to several forms of mass transit—111 South Wacker was the first in the world to achieve LEED core-and-shell Gold certification. Enveloped in high-performance glass that allows natural light to infuse the space without causing excessive heat gain, and replete with integrated green roofs, the building is composed mostly of materials that were manufactured close to the job site. Additionally, many of the materials were chosen for their recycled content, and construction refuse was kept almost entirely out of landfills. Provisions were made for alternative-fuel cars in the parking garage, which also features bike storage areas, encouraging eco-sensitive lifestyles both in and out of the office.

Environmentally responsible materials were specified to enhance the air quality, which translates to healthier, happier, more productive employees. It has been said that more than 75 percent of a tenant's expenses are allocated for labor; therefore, creating a healthful environment that minimizes employees' sick days and augments the way they view their employer—as an entity that truly cares—both increases team members' level of comfort and enhances the company's bottom line. Buildings like 111 South Wacker have pioneered the way for the development of sustainable projects; in fact, many of the nation's foremost companies choose to office exclusively in LEED-certified structures.

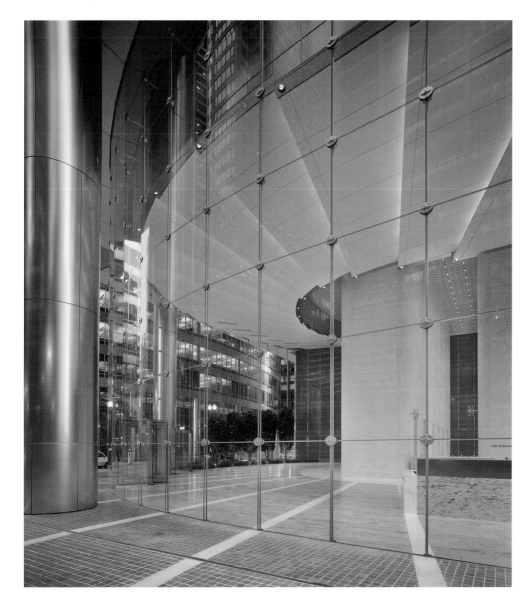

With the ever-increasing price of commodities, and rents that inch up but never quite meet the cost of construction, the challenge climbs greater with each project: to design great architecture, built impeccably at a value no one would have guessed. This philosophy has not only impelled the architects of Goettsch Partners to stay on the lookout for crossover uses of new substances, interesting applications of tried-and-true materials and creative ways to finish or construct their designs, it has also resulted in buildings like 111 South Wacker being leased and sold in record time. The structure's exquisite lobby, which is enclosed by special non-reflective glass that is cleverly suspended from vertical cables, truly echoes the profound impact it has had on the city's intricate tapestry. ■ ■ ■ ■ ■ ■ ■ ■ ■ ■

ABOVE LEFT: The lobby's ultra-transparent glass wall allows the indoor and outdoor areas to be perceived as a single, continuous space.
Photograph by James Steinkamp Photography

ABOVE RIGHT: The openness of the lobby is enhanced by the cable-supported glass enclosure.
Photograph by James Steinkamp Photography

FACING PAGE LEFT: The project's design combines the structural and architectural elements into a consistent expression that emphasizes verticality.
Photograph by James Steinkamp Photography

FACING PAGE RIGHT: At night, the 53-story building appears to float on its illuminated base.
Photograph by James Steinkamp Photography

340 on the Park

■ ■

Solomon Cordwell Buenz

■ ■ ■ ■ ■ ■ ■ ■ ■ For designers at Solomon Cordwell Buenz, each high-rise residential project is treated as an opportunity to enhance the quality of urban life, incorporate sustainable technology and make a statement about living in the modern age.

These were the driving forces behind 340 on the Park. At 62 stories, 340 on the Park is the tallest all-residential tower in Chicago, and the first in the Midwestern United States to meet LEED Silver certification. As such, 340 on the Park has sustainable standards that include an efficient, unitized curtainwall, green roofs, and sophisticated management systems, features that allow the building to operate using 10 percent less source energy than a conventionally designed building of the same size.

FACING PAGE: An overall aerial view of 340 on the Park shows the inspiration for its name.
Photograph by James Steinkamp Photography

340 on the Park pioneered green design for a structure of its type, size and scale, but the form came from the building's spectacular setting: a prominent site at the north end of Grant Park in the heart of Chicago's cultural center. Principal in charge of design Martin Wolf envisioned a predominantly glass tower capitalizing on views overlooking the park, the lake and the city. The tower's distinctive, prow-shaped profile is oriented for optimal sightlines in all directions, with special emphasis toward the lake. Glass is the key element giving character to the exterior form. Planes of floor-to-ceiling glass are combined with a framework of metal panels to create a deep matrix of space, within which are positioned arrays of balconies on the south and north façades.

A winter garden on the 25th floor serves as a light-filled common area for all of the residents of 340 on the Park, and is flanked to the south by an outdoor terrace that overlooks the city and lake below. This two-story interior garden opens through 14-foot-tall glass doors to the exterior space, allowing residents open air and the spectacular vista to the south. Other common amenities on the floor include a fitness room, a two-lane lap pool and a lounge, all treated as a suite of open spaces sharing a common 20-foot ceiling.

At ground level, the design of the tower features an undulating glass envelope that encloses the lobby and celebrates views to the street, offering a graceful transition between the entry space and the spectacular outdoor setting. This successful evolution of cutting-edge architecture and sustainable innovations affirms SCB's place at the forefront of the most current trends in high-rise residential design. ■ ■ ■ ■ ■ ■ ■ ■ ■ ■

ABOVE LEFT: The winter garden on the 25th floor is a common space with a spectacular view.
Photograph by James Steinkamp Photography

ABOVE RIGHT: A view into the lobby shows the vast planes of glass and fine woodworking inside.
Photograph by James Steinkamp Photography

FACING PAGE LEFT: From the north, 340 on the Park knife-edges to maximize the view of Lake Michigan.
Photograph by David B. Seide, © Defined Space

FACING PAGE RIGHT: Balconies jut sharply from the south side of the building.
Photograph by David B. Seide, © Defined Space

Exelon Corporation Corporate Headquarters

Epstein

■ ■ ■ ■ ■ ■ ■ ■ ■ One of the largest energy companies in the United States, Exelon Corporation continually reinvents itself as the premier energy provider, with reliability—keeping the lights on—and responsibility—clean, efficient production. With the new millennium came an interest in pursuing not only the latest technologies in the field, as it were, but also the latest in conscientious design at Exelon's corporate headquarters in downtown Chicago. When Exelon's intentions became public, Epstein took its long history of understanding visions and brought a new design scheme to Exelon. The product of this combining of energies resulted in the LEED-CI Platinum, 250,000-square-foot headquarters—a model of efficient design.

FACING PAGE: Beyond the café window lies Lake Michigan, the pinnacle of Chicago views.
Project Design Team: Susan Jacobson and Stella Volkman.
Photograph by Steve Hall

At 10 floors, the Exelon building is a consolidation of offices, with design schemes that needed to link thematically forward-thinking and traditional elements, and function with public and private mechanisms in tandem—all in one cohesive message. The question was what to say through the space. It was very clear to the team at Epstein that modernist aesthetics—with specific attention paid to the LEED components—would commingle with a twist on some classic coloration. Exelon's vision was a clean, modern, universal building that would offer a variety of experiences for those traveling through. Walking the wide corridors, one may notice open office spaces that promote communication; certain warm and cool color palettes throughout have a high range of values for visual relief: a little orange, say, for energy to complement the gray tones.

The design team really stretched to reach LEED certification. Some 90-percent of lighting is natural—open perimeters not only enhance aesthetics but ensure abundant natural light; low-VOC materials were manufactured locally or were of recycled content; water consumption is reduced through careful planning of the plumbing system; Exelon even reused some of the furniture from its old building. Planning for a long future in downtown Chicago, Exelon was able to commit to the creation of a high-performance building.

Design is a powerful tool. Consequently, you are what you portray. Committed to seeing Exelon's plan through, Epstein set the tone for the corporate headquarters through a series of "visioning sessions," wherein the design team could find the specifics of Exelon's image. Being responsible neighbors was of high priority, but the employees reap their own rewards—along with great Chicago views from the work spaces, Exelon put a workout room in the building. This is productive energy. ■ ■ ■ ■ ■ ■ ■ ■ ■ ■

ABOVE: The executive boardroom radiates a technical efficiency.
Photograph by Steve Hall

TOP RIGHT: Photography of the Exelon power site collection brightens the executive corridor.
Photograph by Steve Hall

BOTTOM RIGHT: The executive reception offers both cool and warm tones through material choice.
Photograph by Steve Hall

FACING PAGE TOP: Open office workstations flank the enclosed office sliding door fronts.
Photograph by Steve Hall

FACING PAGE BOTTOM: A standard open office workstation has a warming color palette to offset the traditional scheme.
Photograph by Steve Hall

Harm A. Weber Academic Center

■ ■

Burnidge Cassell Associates

■ ■ ■ ■ ■ ■ ■ ■ ■ ■ In 2004 Judson University held an international design competition for a new building to house the Library and Division of Art, Design and Architecture. As architect of record, Burnidge Cassell Associates worked with Short and Associates of London to create an innovative 88,000-square-foot building with a sustainable focus. The driving concept utilizes passive solar techniques and the thermal behavior of air to naturally heat and ventilate the four-story building. Solid precast concrete panels provide thermal mass, capturing radiant heat from the sun. The heat is released to warm the air in cool weather and retained to cool the building on warmer days. Fresh air is drawn in through large dampers at the building's base. As the air temperature increases, it naturally rises and is circulated to the floors before being discharged through roof-level turrets.

FACING PAGE: The south façade of the academic center is topped with photovoltaic panels to induce vertical air circulation and overlooks the detention area and native plantings.
Project Design Team: Richard C. McCarthy, Charles H. Burnidge, James A. Enck, C. Alan Short and Wade Ross.
Photograph by Bruce Starrenburg, Lightbox Digital

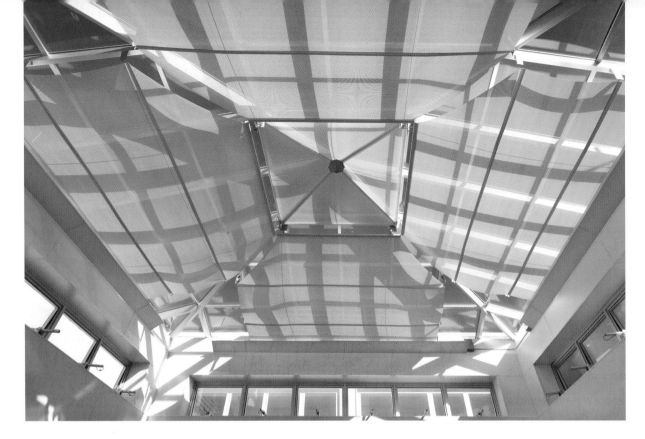

Ventilation occurs in the library section through a central atrium crowned by a glazed "greenhouse" space. This "greenhouse" heats the air, creating thermal lift, pulling it through the atrium to be distributed to the library spaces. The office wing is topped by an attic lined with photovoltaic panels. In addition to producing energy, residual heat from the photovoltaic panels increases the attic temperature, accelerating the natural ventilation in this portion of the building. Air circulates through shafts expressed on the building's exterior. A mechanical system is provided when the temperature and humidity exceed predetermined set points, surpassing the natural ventilation system's capabilities. The sun is also used to decrease the need for artificial illumination. Narrow floor plates maximize the penetration of sunlight into rooms, while large upper panes allow light to enter high on the wall, creating a rich, uniform effect. Lower, operable "view" windows allow individual thermal control and the psychological benefit of a visual connection with the natural environment. The Harm A. Weber Academic Center presents an alternative philosophy, focusing on building sustainability. With the design based on natural phenomena, the center closes the gap between the built environment and nature. Judson University has created a prototype for the next generation of sustainable buildings that fulfills its mission of being a good steward of the Earth and a leader in education. ■ ■ ■ ■ ■ ■ ■ ■ ■ ■

TOP LEFT: Computer-controlled blinds shield the central atrium from unwanted solar gain.
Photograph by Bruce Starrenburg, Lightbox Digital

BOTTOM LEFT: Air enters the atrium through a plenum located between the glass floor and the second level. It then circulates throughout the spaces by means of mechanically operated clerestory windows.
Photograph by Bruce Starrenburg, Lightbox Digital

FACING PAGE TOP: The four-story building is divided into three sections. The center academic section links the library and architectural studios to an elongated office and fine arts wing.
Photograph by Bruce Starrenburg, Lightbox Digital

FACING PAGE BOTTOM: Building details left to right: roof level exhaust turret; fenestration at central stair; individualized window surrounds for solar control; central atrium.
Photographs by Bruce Starrenburg, Lightbox Digital

The Merchandise Mart

■ ■

Merchandise Mart Properties, Inc.

■ ■ ■ ■ ■ ■ ■ ■ ■ When a 4.2 million-square-foot building erected in the 1920s achieves LEED-EB Silver certification, heads turn. Joseph P. Kennedy acquired The Merchandise Mart in 1945 and transformed it into the country's foremost tradeshow venue—his grandson Christopher Kennedy has passionately continued to build upon that legacy. Though reaching LEED status would signify a finish line to most, Chris and his associates see it as just the beginning.

Green has always made sense to The Mart's leadership and tenants, who have championed recycling, energy efficiency and healthful finishes and cleaning products since long before sustainability was in vogue. Demonstrative of "The Mart Way" of doing everything better, faster and more uniquely, Merchandise Mart Properties set its sights on the highest honor awarded by USGBC to existing architecture. A building-wide survey documented extant eco-conscious practices, and then a team of architects, engineers and other consultants developed a plan to boost the historic building to a level of

FACING PAGE: Sustainability is a way of life at The Merchandise Mart, the world's largest LEED-EB certified building.
Photograph by Steven Dahlman

environmental friendliness that even new construction would envy. Chris and his team cite their ability to get people excited, on board and continually involved in sustainable practices as the key to the project's success. On top of requisite improvements—installing low-watt fixtures and motion sensors; landscaping with drought-tolerant plants; maintaining the underground thermal storage system; and expanding the recycling program to encompass cardboard, construction materials, light bulbs, batteries, aluminum and glass—they have thought up sincerely clever ways to keep people interested. Among them are a car-sharing program, a standing offer of free admission to consumer events by showing a bicycle helmet, simple guidelines for minimizing waste at events, and education programs for tenants, special interest groups and the public.

The Mart hosts hundreds of high-end tradeshows, consumer shows and charity events each year, welcoming a staggering 20,000 visitors on a daily basis to enter its façade of 29 million bricks and 4,000 windows. Producing Merchandise Mart Properties' Art Chicago requires the hands of some 80 carpenters, 40 painters, 20 electricians and various other tradespeople; it involves roughly 70 art handlers who receive art from 180 dealers from more than 30 countries. The incredible magnitude of happenings at The Mart underscores the importance of fine-tuning every detail with sustainability foremost in mind. One small change effected throughout a building with its own zip code yields significant results.

Complementing The Mart's Silver status, a number of the tenant designer showrooms, boutiques, retail shops and office have followed suit in green pursuits of their own—many achieving LEED-CI certification. To stay ahead of the curve, a team of senior engineers and property managers meet biweekly to brainstorm and devise innovative plans for furthering their collective eco-conscious mission. Recertifying the building every five years will be mere routine. It is the hope of all involved with The Mart that their dedication will inspire building owners, city leaders, architects and engineers around the globe to follow suit.

ABOVE: *Five Lights in the Valley*, a painted urethane sculpture by celebrated contemporary artist Jim Dine, was installed in the south lobby during Art Chicago. Courtesy of Richard Gray Gallery of Chicago and New York, the piece is one of more than two dozen temporary public art installations in and around The Merchandise Mart.
Photograph by Paul Audia

FACING PAGE TOP: *Simple Elegance*, designed by Barbara Barry for Kravet and Henredon, was one of nine luxury living spaces created for the yearly Dream Rooms at The Merchandise Mart.
Photograph by Gordon Beall

FACING PAGE BOTTOM: The grand lobby of The Merchandise Mart is crowned by Jules Guerin's frieze of murals depicting commerce throughout the world.
Photograph by Don Horne

Tuthill Corporate Headquarters

████ ████ ████ ████ ████ ████ ████ ████ ████ ████ ████ ████ ████ ████ ████ ████ ████

Serena Sturm Architects, Ltd.

■ ■ ■ ■ ■ ■ ■ ■ ■ ■ A company's headquarters should exude strength, durability and make a statement about the organization's integrity. As Tuthill Corporation—a fourth-generation family-owned manufacturing business—saw its market expanding, the consensus was that a new headquarters and training center was needed. Leadership believed that the architecture had to not only engage current and future employees but also give clients a tangible vision of success gained without compromising context. Serena Sturm Architects delivered that statement through a holistic design scheme well-ahead of environmental building trends at the time.

ABOVE: The main entrance passes through the caretaker's housing.
Photograph by Serena Sturm Architects

FACING PAGE: The central commons surrounding an indoor pond is used for work and leisure activities.
Photograph by Barry Rustin Photography

For more than 25 years, Serena Sturm Architects has been building for tomorrow and the Tuthill Corporate Headquarters was no different. The designers knew that the features that create an inspiring, healthy workplace get paid for by increased user productivity, and that finding the highest levels of comfort for employees would lead to achievement. A primary goal was to validate the science behind pioneering building technology used to enhance staff performance. The building's integration into the site was the first priority. Through the power of a very contemporary envelope, Tuthill Corporate Headquarters harnesses nature's assets and protects against its excesses. Nestled into a hill, the shell minimizes its exposure to harsher elements like winter winds, while opening shaded glass to the southern sun and the site's most precious view. Expansive daylighting—the always preferable cousin to the fluorescent bulb—floods deep into the building, which utilizes an automated dimming system to control electrical lighting when appropriate. Such techniques result in nature moving people through the building.

But the building's uniqueness is not only in the art of the design or the minimal consumption of energy; the construction materials required have also been minimized through standardization. As the floorplan was designed in modules, a centipede-like quality produces the slight curvature of the modules, where the points of curvature are reserved for supply rooms, restrooms and other support spaces. This means that any addition to the building can be integrated quickly and efficiently. This interest in conserving floor-plate size developed a morphing theme to the building—accentuated by a request for a dual-use auditorium/ training room, which birthed a hydraulic floor that can go from auditorium to dead level in five minutes.

Setting a new direction for the Tuthill Corporation also allowed Serena Sturm Architects to set a new direction for the site. The site had not been maintained, and so working with a team of landscape consultants, Serena Sturm Architects cleared invasive species, eliminated curbs to filter stormwater into the landscape, and collected roof runoff in subgrade perforated pipe to recharge groundwater. The natural prairie landscape now promotes use. Nature walks and outdoor spaces are no longer solely break spots, but rather they are incorporated into the work day. Tuthill Corporate Headquarters encourages an environmental stand that is not just about conserving energy or being nature's steward, but is about how a building should serve its occupants well. ■ ■ ■ ■ ■ ■ ■ ■ ■ ■

TOP LEFT: Art, architecture and nature are blended to heighten the employee experience.
Photograph by Barry Rustin Photography

TOP RIGHT: Landscaped terraces, dining patios and a balcony connect indoor and outdoor uses.
Photograph by Barry Rustin Photography

FACING PAGE TOP: Flexible open office settings bathed in daylight receive services from a raised floor.
Photograph by Barry Rustin Photography

FACING PAGE BOTTOM: The reception is part of a northern entrance terrace that pierces through southern glass.
Photograph by Barry Rustin Photography

Vernon Hills Village Hall

Yas Architecture, LLC

■ ■ ■ ■ ■ ■ ■ ■ ■ A successful community building should evolve from the cultural and traditional values of the community. Stephen Yas, AIA, RIBA, approached the Vernon Hills Village Hall design process with no preconceived notions. The design was a patient search and a path of discovery based upon the client's program and the historic symbolism found within the community. It was upon these principals that YAS Architecture—formerly Yas/Fischel Partnership—was founded: "Before there is a concept, there must be a spirit."

Vernon Hills was originally a farming community, so Stephen drew inspiration from the rustic materials of old barn structures, reinterpreting them into a modern design rooted in the past but reaching for the future. Additionally, the planners wanted the design to convey to the community that they are always

working on its behalf. This effect was achieved through the lighting design that, at night, illuminates the council chamber and symbolizes the elected officials as a beacon of light to the community.

The building form, and its use of materials, delineates between the legislative branch of government and the administrative branch. The administrative section of the building is comprised of two distinctly different materials that balance each other in texture and tone. The updated barn wood tucks seamlessly beneath aluminum reveals, and the lannon stone elevates to the wood, referencing local barn structures. Vast panels of glass allow much more natural light into the interior than the original building and complete the modern combination of aluminum and natural wood. The legislative branch, depicted by the council chamber, is comprised of three walls of fritted glass, metal panels and a perforated metal fascia, and symbolizes the elected officials reaching for the future.

Stephen desired to create a living building, designing a grove of trees at the entrance to give the impression of an orchard on the original farmland. Giant limestone slabs serve as benches and, when vacant, look like something culled from a farm, rather than an empty seat.

LEFT: The office wing view details the blending of old and new.
Photograph by Chris Barrett, Hedrich Blessing Photography

FACING PAGE TOP: The council chamber is basked in natural light that flows through fritted glass, a green design element.
Photograph by Chris Barrett, Hedrich Blessing Photography

FACING PAGE BOTTOM: White "clouds" reflect light in this hallway-lobby to the manager's office.
Photograph by Chris Barrett, Hedrich Blessing Photography

The green aspects of the Vernon Hills Village Hall were planned with precision. Along with natural slate, cobblestones and a natural wooden canopy, the stormwater detention requirement was designed to look like a naturally occurring pond on a farm with prairie grasses along its perimeter, giving the impression that the building was designed around this body of water.

In the council chamber, the large glass panels are fritted with a pattern of one-inch white squares that ultimately reduce ultraviolet rays by 50 percent. In the public library and corridor, "clouds" of white drywall are hung from the ceiling as reflectors for upturned lights, which utilize the ceiling as a light reflector to reduce energy. Paramount in YAS Architecture's design is the concept of modern architecture with tactile materials and green initiative.

Reinventing the function of this civic center required a careful mix of program elements including a village hall, a senior center and a branch public library in the lower level. The library is housed in space for future municipal expansion. Stephen sees citizen involvement in the design process as a necessity, for true civic structures have many uses. The result is a building crafted not just by YAS Architecture, but also by the people of Vernon Hills. ■ ■ ■ ■ ■ ■ ■ ■ ■ ■

CHAPTER SIX
City Futures

If a modern-day city sprung up through the creative genius of one architect alone—regardless of how talented he or she may be—it would pale in comparison to one that evolved over decades, even centuries, and was touched by the hands of many. The most spectacular cities in the world boast an eclectic mixture of architectural styles, from classical to contemporary, and it is the architect's prerogative to reinvent these broad genres to tailor a building's aesthetic appearance and functionality to the current and future needs of those who will interact with it on a daily basis.

A great deal of trust and communication is required for a group of people to conceptualize and develop plans for works of architecture that may not be tangibly built until many years down the road. Lucien Lagrange Architects' X|O, Antheus Capital and Studio Gang Architects' Solstice on the Park, and Weiss Architects' PURE are a few illustrious examples. The collective realized visions of past architects provide an exquisite tapestry into which the masterpieces we call contemporary art may be harmoniously woven.

Enjoy these products of research, inspiration and diligence that will culminate in buildings yet to be constructed. Take a glimpse of what is yet to come through these dynamic drawings, blueprints and renderings.

Block 37, Joseph Freed and Associates LLC, page 280

The Legacy at Millennium Park, Mesa Development, LLC, Walsh Investors, LLC, page 284

Trump International Hotel & Tower Chicago, Skidmore, Owings & Merrill LLP, page 304

455 North Park Drive Hotel and Residences

Fordham Company

■ ■ ■ ■ ■ ■ ■ ■ ■ ■ There is a tremendous residential renaissance taking place in downtown Chicago. Many major new buildings are going up—many are modern structures that lean to a new millennium; a few are traditional Gold Coast structures that reflect old Chicago. Either way, Chicago is certainly continuing its century-long status as one of the greatest architectural cities of the world, and Fordham Company is certainly carrying its weight. An exclusively high-end residential developer, Christopher T. Carley, founder of Fordham Company, had just launched the development for the Chicago Spire—a 2,000-foot, 150-story residential building designed by Santiago Calatrava—and was looking for another great iconic building in the shadow of the Chicago Spire. A better "next" project than 455 North Park Drive Hotel Residences could rarely be found.

Wanting no Son of Spire—because of its sheer proximity to the other project—Christopher desired a tall, slender, elegant building that could perhaps tip its hat to the Spire's twisting nature. This nod exists at the hotel's top. With a traditional square base, 455 North Park Drive shoots up 1,230 feet, tapering two opposite corners like a scalpel at the roof. As the building begins to taper, it appears to slightly twist—the salute to its rotary neighbor. In this association, both of these structures confidently propel the Streeterville community into its new status as the preeminent high-rise neighborhood and make significant marks on the Chicago skyline.

This sleek structure carefully divides 104 floors between its five-star hotel and some of the finest, most-varied residencies in the country; and a Louis Vuitton spa—the 29th and 30th floors—seems like a good dividing line. Above this are 300 luxury residences, one to three bedrooms at the large average of 1,800 square feet. Twenty-eight-foot glass spans ensure that the unobstructed views are spectacular. The open plan calls for dimensions that have no columns and 10-foot ceilings. And for the visitor to Chicago, the 350 hotel rooms at the base propel a mission of sheer elegance.

With this building the pull will be worldwide, an international, architectural icon. Being that 455 North Park Drive will be one of the tallest buildings in the world, its impact will be astounding. Just east of the Magnificent Mile, steps from the Chicago River and Lake Michigan, the building is likewise enmeshed in one of the most affluent neighborhoods in the nation. Fortunately, Christopher and Fordham Company know how to develop exceptionally beautiful residential and hospitality edifices. ■ ■ ■ ■ ■ ■ ■ ■ ■ ■

RIGHT: The landscaping and iconic pyramid canopy will enhance the pedestrian experience as they draw people to the hotel entrance and into the park.
Rendering by ImageFiction

FACING PAGE TOP: Looking west down the Ogden Slip, 455 North Park Drive's slender form dramatically defines the view corridor to the Tribune Tower.
Rendering by DeStefano and Partners

FACING PAGE BOTTOM: The hotel's glass entry pavilion gracefully establishes a sense of arrival while dramatically maintaining the openness of the park and view corridor, looking west to Lake Michigan.
Rendering by ImageFiction

Block 37

Joseph Freed and Associates LLC

For 20 years Block 37, in the heart of downtown Chicago, has lain dormant. Several attempts to develop this difficult site have failed. However, Joseph Freed and Associates has been able to meet the challenges of trying to excavate and build on a single city block without a total disruption of the traffic and life of the central city. Block 37 is a key element in the revitalization of State Street and offers an exciting mix of retail, dining and entertainment options for downtown office workers, the large student population in the area, Chicago residents and visitors to the city.

The City of Chicago engaged in an extensive and intense planning process to devise the appropriate methods to be used to select the master developer for this site and to then work with that developer to plan the project in what has become a historic example of a public-private partnership in Chicago.

ABOVE: The Marshall Field's clock is just one of the few historic landmarks that Block 37 is sited amongst.
Rendering by Gensler Architecture

FACING PAGE: Presenting an exciting new façade to State Street, Block 37 is destined to become Chicago's most prominent downtown landmark.
Rendering by Gensler Architecture

The original developer, The Mills Corporation, broke ground for the project in November of 2006. Since then, Joseph Freed and Associates has taken over the project and now leads the development.

This is a phased project. The office tower, located at the corner of Dearborn and Washington, is being built by Golub & Company. The tenants include the global headquarters of Morningstar and the CBS 2 Chicago television station and corporate offices. The second phase of the project is the retail portion, scheduled to open in the spring of 2009 with an exciting mix of retail, dining and entertainment options for Chicagoans and visitors alike, followed with a hotel and residential component to be built atop the retail space.

The style of the project is reflective and intended to complement and embrace the diverse neighborhoods and architecture found on each side of the project. On the north, the project fronts on the city's famed theater district, with planned restaurants and the hotel entrance to encourage interaction with the theaters. The west side faces Daley Plaza, with its government office buildings and The Chicago Picasso. The office tower and CBS Channel 2 studios will complement that exposure. The south side is part of the city's business and office life and the entrance to Block 37's office complex. And the east side is State Street. And here, vision is the theme—from inside patrons can see out to iconic structures, like the Marshall Field's Clock, while from the outside pedestrians can see the activity and merchandise inside.

TOP LEFT: Spectacular atrium views are provided from the bustling transit level for commuters and visitors.
Rendering by Gensler Architecture

BOTTOM LEFT: The Dearborn Street elevation shows retail and restaurants on the left and the new office center with CBS Channel 2 studios on the right.
Rendering by Gensler Architecture

Block 37 will be the heart of Chicago's central city. It is a 24/7 location, offering visitors, residents, office workers and students an exciting range of shopping, dining and entertainment adjacent to State Street, as well as to the city's theaters, its cultural institutions and Millennium Park. ■ ■ ■ ■ ■ ■ ■ ■ ■ ■

ABOVE LEFT: A unique vantage point from Level 2 features storefronts and LED boards on each level.
Rendering by Gensler Architecture

ABOVE RIGHT: CBS Channel 2 studios will become a gathering place for visitors, shoppers and office workers in The Loop.
Rendering by Gensler Architecture

The Legacy at Millennium Park

■ ■

Mesa Development, LLC
Walsh Investors, LLC

■ ■ ■ ■ ■ ■ ■ ■ ■ ■ One of the key components to urban residential architecture is considering the lifestyle of the residents who will eventually call the building home. Five years after their Heritage at Millennium Park project—a classic residential tower—Mesa Development and Walsh Investors set their eyes on a new site, just three blocks south of The Heritage. Responding to the evolving downtown luxury residential market, the team sought to create a building that satisfied the market's appetite for modern architecture while satisfying buyers' demands for world-class amenities and uninterrupted views of Lake Michigan and Millennium Park. With these goals in mind, Mesa Development and Walsh Investors created the tall, airy, light and thin Legacy at Millennium Park, utilizing the same talented crew as its previous building, including Solomon Cordwell Buenz for the architectural design and Walsh Construction as the general contractor. The Legacy will live up to its name, for its stunning façade will surely endure.

FACING PAGE: Rising above Millennium Park and the lakefront, The Legacy will take its place in Chicago's legacy of great architecture.
Rendering by ImageFiction

Sitting on less than an acre at the south end of Millennium Park, The Legacy rises 73 stories with a sophisticated glass and metal curtainwall. The unique shape of the slender tower allows for gorgeous views to Millennium Park and Lake Michigan from nearly every residential unit. As well, the all-glass façade displays an ever-changing design, reflecting the sky, the park and the lake in all of their differing moods. Whether it is a gorgeous sunrise over the lake or a dramatic summer sunset over the city skyline, residents of The Legacy have the perfect opportunity to experience the Chicago vista.

Chicago is known as a city with an abundance of green space, from the string of lakefront parks that line almost the entire shore of Lake Michigan to the many neighborhood parks that define the city. In keeping with this tradition, the design team of The Legacy has created parks in the sky to service this vertical neighborhood. A landscaped deck on the 15th floor of the tower provides space for residents to relax and enjoy the outdoors. Skydeck lounges on the 42nd and 60th floors offer indoor and outdoor areas where residents can enjoy the stunning views from a more elevated perspective.

LEFT: The Legacy rises above the historic Michigan Avenue street wall.
Rendering by ImageFiction

FACING PAGE LEFT: The Legacy provides breathtaking views of Millennium Park's numerous cultural offerings.
Photograph by James Steinkamp Photography

FACING PAGE RIGHT: Buckingham Fountain, Adler Planetarium, the John G. Shedd Aquarium and Monroe Harbor are visible from The Legacy.
Photograph by Skorbury & Associates

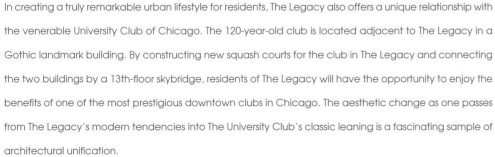

In creating a truly remarkable urban lifestyle for residents, The Legacy also offers a unique relationship with the venerable University Club of Chicago. The 120-year-old club is located adjacent to The Legacy in a Gothic landmark building. By constructing new squash courts for the club in The Legacy and connecting the two buildings by a 13th-floor skybridge, residents of The Legacy will have the opportunity to enjoy the benefits of one of the most prestigious downtown clubs in Chicago. The aesthetic change as one passes from The Legacy's modern tendencies into The University Club's classic leaning is a fascinating sample of architectural unification.

The ability for developers to form relationships in creating neighborhoods is essential in long-term planning, and The Legacy at Millennium Park is not only a remarkable structure and a great neighbor, but it makes a perfect modern-to-classic bookend to Mesa Development's other Millennium Park event, The Heritage. ■ ■ ■ ■ ■ ■ ■ ■ ■ ■ ■

Mandarin Oriental, Chicago

Solomon Cordwell Buenz

■ ■ ■ ■ ■ ■ ■ ■ ■ ■ At 75 stories, the 1.3-million-square-foot Mandarin Oriental, Chicago rises from the emerging downtown neighborhood of Chicago's East Loop and is convenient to both Millennium Park and Michigan Avenue. The 833-foot-tall tower is a modern composition of richly detailed contemporary materials that architecturally embodies the quality of the Mandarin Oriental brand within the existing urban fabric.

Facing east and south to capitalize on views to the lake and to the park, the tower includes 252 luxury hotel rooms and suites, 103 branded residences and 161 private condominiums. Within the building's 13-story base are amenities supporting the luxurious atmosphere: a 32,000-square-foot signature spa, upscale restaurants and retail, 12,000 square feet of meeting space, two ballrooms—including the largest five-star ballroom in the city—recreation and fitness areas and six floors of aboveground parking for residents. Below grade are four levels of valet parking for hotel guests and a concourse with glass-

FACING PAGE: At street level, the base of Mandarin Oriental, Chicago suggests promising things to come.
Rendering by Manic Image

enclosed bridges, escalators and walkways linking the Mandarin Oriental to shops in the existing concourse level of Two Illinois Centre, the Lake Shore Athletic Club and retail on North Michigan Avenue.

At street level, shops and restaurants reinforce the pedestrian ambience, while hotel guests and residents access their respective areas of the building through separate entrances. From the hotel porte-cochere and ground-floor lobby, express elevators deliver guests to hotel reception at the sky-lobby on the 11th floor, 170 feet above ground. Monumental glass walls at the sky-lobby celebrate the spectacular views from reception, lounge, restaurant and bar to Millennium Park and Lake Michigan.

The exterior form takes advantage of modern glass technology to create a sophisticated, consistent wrapper for the wide variety of functions taking place within the mass of the building. The tower, containing the hotel rooms and condominiums, is expressed as a sleek glass form split into two volumes. The volume facing the lake is articulated as a thin prism of glass; the volume facing west defers to this taller element as it "peels" back in a graceful arc to reveal the luminous lantern at the top of the tower.

At the base, the east façade is comprised of a combination of translucent glass, vision glass and projecting horizontal blades to disguise the parking levels and to visually unify this component with the hotel function floors above. The west façade, screening the service components of the hotel, is treated as a vertical metal plane that rises to the sky-lobby level, and then folds over to become the roof of the sky-lobby functions. A series of ocular skylights punctuate the roof to add light to the restaurant and animate the exterior deck.

Designed by noted architectural firm Solomon Cordwell Buenz, this mixed-use, five-star hotel and residential tower is a vertical city within the city. ■ ■ ■ ■ ■ ■ ■ ■ ■ ■

ABOVE: This condominium living room offers one-of-a-kind views of Lake Michigan.
Rendering by Neoscope

FACING PAGE LEFT: The exterior is a fascinating study of modern architecture.
Rendering by Manic Image

FACING PAGE TOP: Interiors at Mandarin Oriental are by Avery Brooks & Associates, as seen in the Sky Lobby.
Rendering by Neoscope

FACING PAGE BOTTOM: The Mandarin Restaurant offers meals of exceptional quality.
Rendering by Neoscope

PURE

■ ■

Weiss Architects, LLC

■ ■ ■ ■ ■ ■ ■ ■ ■ ■ So much of architectural design is problem-solving. When Sunrise Equities bought the property that would become PURE condominiums, the company asked Steve Weiss of Weiss Architects to review some of the possible problems that might be faced when building. Steve immediately saw the potential of this great Chicago neighborhood and soon became the principal architect on the project.

This 68-unit condominium building reinvigorates the old mill neighborhood by pushing an unusual design for the locality: PURE has a nearly all-glass exterior, which creates a portrait for glances to downtown Chicago. Having large areas of glass means that not only are interiors lively and pronounced, but views of the city skyline from these window walls are maximized. As the residences sit atop three stories of parking, this garage space is day-lit for energy savings with tall glass walls and with convenient retail spaces incorporated in the base.

FACING PAGE: PURE opens up to Morgan Street, placing a well-proportioned glass prism on a concrete and glass podium.
Project Design Team: Steve Weiss, Ryan White, Caitlin Carey, Ted Lampa and Betsy Scherrer.
Rendering by Weiss Architects, LLC

But building shape played a major role. This very calculated building employs an L-shaped plan, which serves two purposes: to maximize views out and to let natural light in, creating a building that is light and open. Though PURE does relate to adjacent buildings, it is not contextual. While being a tad taller than the buildings in context, PURE is designed as a very crisp and cool structure, contrasting with the ponderous masonry buildings nearby. Here lies Weiss Architect's expertise: intensive focus on precision.

In close collaboration with Sunrise, Weiss Architects designed a highly energy-efficient building. The window walls use energy-saving glass, and by thorough analysis and design of all the units, sustainable materials were used throughout, including flooring and finishes. But the overriding design purpose of PURE is to create something iconic: a building all in the modernist tradition. Steve Weiss has managed to imbue his best proficiencies onto a great site in the River West neighborhood, for PURE becomes a fine example of maximizing architectural potential. ■ ■ ■ ■ ■ ■ ■ ■ ■ ■

TOP LEFT: Interior spaces are light and open, finished with sustainable materials.
Rendering by Weiss Architects, LLC

BOTTOM LEFT: The roof of the parking garage has large, landscaped terraces for communal use.
Rendering by Weiss Architects, LLC

FACING PAGE LEFT: The precision of the design is evident in the detailing of the concrete, glass and metal materials of PURE's exterior.
Rendering by Weiss Architects, LLC

FACING PAGE RIGHT: PURE is well-proportioned and well-sited to contrast with and yet fit into the River West neighborhood.
Rendering by Weiss Architects, LLC

Schaumburg Center for the Performing Arts

■■■■■■■■■■■■■■■■■■■■■■■■■■■■■■■■■■■

Daniel P. Coffey & Associates, Ltd.

■■■■■■■■■ Although acknowledged for his designs of many types of projects—from mixed-use towers to subways to unique department stores—Daniel P. Coffey, FAIA, is perhaps best known in Chicago as the recognized expert for the design of performing arts facilities. His work in this arena includes multiple venues in the region and around the country, including massive renovations and bold, ground-up centers.

When the dynamic "edge city" of Schaumburg, Illinois, decided to commission a new performing arts center, it knew Daniel was the architect to retain. Known for quality design work and attention to both aesthetic and functional detail, Daniel was to create a bold landmark that would properly position Schaumburg as a cultural center for Chicago's northwestern suburban area.

FACING PAGE: From the air, the conical sheath singles out the theater.
Rendering by Daniel P. Coffey & Associates, Ltd.

The new performing arts center is located on the Northwest Tollway, adjacent to the newly constructed, city-owned Renaissance Convention Center and Hotel. The prominent site was very visible but handicapped by its generally being seen at 70 miles per hour.

The goal, therefore, was to grab visual attention at the large, high-speed scale of the highway, make a memorable impression and then translate that boldness to the intimate scale of a theatrical venue as one walks up to and enters the center.

The designed result is a stunning success, where a bold but transparent exterior cover in the form of a truncated cone is placed over and around the plain, simple and economical "boxes" of the lobby, audience chamber, stage, dressing rooms, and mechanical fan rooms. The conical "lamp shade" is easy to grasp, yet visually complex as one gets closer. It is simple in its execution: Often assumed to be glazed, the cone is actually fabricated as a series of freestanding, round, load-bearing, white, aluminum tubes that are strapped together horizontally by several "hoopskirt" rings. Together these tie to form an inherently stable and efficient structure that supports itself like the stud-based "balloon frame" of a traditional house. These elements all act to shield yet subtly expose the glass-enclosed lobbies and entry. These public spaces are detailed with a decidedly human scale and focus on warmth of materials and the textures and patterns of details and construction elements.

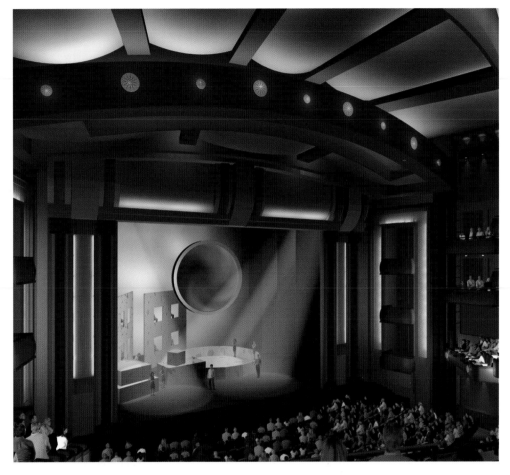

Inside the theater, the stage area is fully outfitted with state-of-the-art theatrical systems and technology. The stage itself is designed to be flexible. Its proscenium arch can change size to accommodate the disparate needs of symphony, Broadway musicals and civic events like political debates and award shows. Similarly, moveable panels on the side and rear walls of the 2,400-seat auditorium can be raised and lowered in various patterns to modify the acoustic environment of the hall and match the requirements of each performance.

Overall, the dynamic new center is an impressive, modern landmark for the Chicago area and will be a destination for audiences of all ages and artistic productions of all types for many years to come. ■ ■ ■ ■

ABOVE LEFT: From the north balcony lobby, the monumental stairs can be seen.
Rendering by Daniel P. Coffey & Associates, Ltd.

ABOVE RIGHT: The Broadway proscenium fronts the auditorium.
Rendering by Daniel P. Coffey & Associates, Ltd.

FACING PAGE TOP: The drop-off zone and main entry reveal the human level of the structure.
Rendering by Daniel P. Coffey & Associates, Ltd.

FACING PAGE BOTTOM: The lobby and lobby bar rest just inside the main entry.
Rendering by Daniel P. Coffey & Associates, Ltd.

Solstice on the Park

■■

Antheus Capital, LLC
Studio Gang Architects

■ ■ ■ ■ ■ ■ ■ ■ ■ Our idea of natural beauty comes from an intrinsic knowledge that a thing's function is the cause of it. A beautiful leaf, for example, looks and feels the way it does because it has to, because it is responding to its environment. Architects today are in a wonderful position to mirror nature—both in beauty and in function—through the advancement of technology and the sheer desire to produce a structure that has an underlying meaning. Solstice on the Park was conceived from this idea. A development of Antheus Capital, with Studio Gang Architects leading the design, Solstice on the Park will prove to be one of Chicago's most interesting responses to site and climate.

FACING PAGE: The building's site in Hyde Park, a historic neighborhood, is just south of Chicago's downtown.
Rendering by Studio Gang Architects

Facing Jackson Park to the south and downtown Chicago to the north, Solstice on the Park is a test in what is appropriate—what ought to be on its site. Jeanne Gang of Studio Gang Architects came to Eli Unger of Antheus Capital with a dazzling proposal to design the aesthetics of this high-rise by responding to the natural forces through the refined tools of modern architecture. Twenty-eight stories tall, this residential tower is shaped around the sun path. Instead of creating sunshades to block the summer sun, the design called for a chiseling of the building. Angled walls expand upward at 71 degrees—the optimum angles for Chicago's latitude. This angle works superbly in winter, for the sun reaches apex below that grade. In other words, the building captures heat in demand, and blocks in surplus.

The performative lateral walls have a strong mathematical overlay. Patterned after the building's structural diagram, these walls reveal their irregularities. Sections not supporting the structure were eliminated—a perforating element that pulls cool air out in winter and warm air out in summer. This in tandem with the heavy use of recycled materials and low-VOC emitting elements, Solstice shoots for LEED Silver certification, but has already been endorsed by preservationists, for the very granular approach to its design ensures a sensitive investment.

Solstice on the Park is designed to reflect how people live today. There are no formal dining rooms with separate kitchens here; the floorplans are takes on the modern inclination toward openness. And for the people amenable to this lifestyle, the building proves a contemporary symbol of functionality. Pay a few moments' attention to this very treelike structure, and the genesis of the idea becomes very clear: There is no better blueprint than nature. ■ ■ ■ ■ ■ ■ ■

RIGHT: The building's angled façade is optimized to reduce solar heat gain in the summer and allow for passive solar heating in the winter. Its exterior shear walls are perforated, responding to the structural forces present inside the wall.
Rendering by ImageFiction

FACING PAGE TOP: Solstice on the Park overlooks Lake Michigan, as well as Chicago's Jackson Park, site of the 1893 Columbian Exposition.
Rendering by FireStar

FACING PAGE BOTTOM: The building's 28 stories respond to the natural forces of Chicago's latitude, while blending with the neighborhood's leafy surroundings.
Rendering by Studio Gang Architects

Trump International Hotel & Tower Chicago

Skidmore, Owings & Merrill LLP

■ ■ ■ ■ ■ ■ ■ ■ ■ ■ For decades, architecture students at the Illinois Institute of Technology viewed the vicinity of 330 North Wabash as somewhat of a dream site for which they sketched, plotted and planned imaginative works of architecture. Though the prime waterfront location has been more than spoken for, as the landmark Trump International Hotel & Tower Chicago is nearly complete, the architecture, far more than its impeccable site, provides an entirely new kind of inspiration. The 92-story Trump Tower establishes a new level of luxury in the hospitality industry, and its innovative design and engineering are of a caliber that architects emerging and seasoned will strive to achieve.

ABOVE: The exceptionally wide spacing of the building's support columns is groundbreaking for designs of this scale yet common among structures a third its size.
Rendering by Crystal CG, © Skidmore, Owings & Merrill LLP

FACING PAGE: The tower's retail and dining components will entice people to linger after hours, adding to the city's vibrancy.
Rendering by Crystal CG, © Skidmore, Owings & Merrill LLP

The Trump Organization selected Skidmore, Owings & Merrill LLP to undertake the challenging architectural and structural design of Chicago's newest landmark. The savvy developer desired a plan with extreme flexibility in order to fleet-footedly respond to the demands of the market. Because of SOM's flexible design, what was originally intended as significant office space with a condominium component was able to evolve into more than 286 finely appointed guestrooms as well as residences with a variety of floorplans, restaurants, retail and amenities such as a world-class spa and health club, without compromising the timetables for completion.

With neighbors like the respected Wrigley and IBM buildings, it was important for Trump Tower to acknowledge its surroundings while making a powerful statement that would echo the level of quality and excellence synonymous with the Trump brand. SOM's team, including managing partner Richard F. Tomlinson II, determined that the surrounding dichotomy of dark buildings, light buildings and the riverfront would be aptly complemented by a material palette of stainless steel and glass to reflect the urban setting's interesting and varied forms. Bill Baker, SOM's partner in charge of structural engineering, eloquently describes the heart of Chicago's majestic skyline as a mountain range and Trump Tower as the peak.

Trump Tower's sheer height gives it tremendous visibility, but the natural way in which Wabash curves around the building allows it to be enjoyed perhaps more wholly and from more vantage points than any other structure in the city. The panoramas from within are equally exhilarating. SOM achieved uninterrupted views through columns spaced at almost unprecedented intervals of 30 feet, about 50 percent wider than most residential buildings.

As Chicago's first building of such a monumental height to be constructed of concrete, Trump Tower is

deeply anchored in a bed of limestone by massive concrete shafts. Its design underwent extensive wind

tunnel testing, and because of the tight site, the project's scale, and the need to seamlessly incorporate

multiple uses, SOM's interdisciplinary design approach was key. Trump International Hotel & Tower

Chicago presents itself as tall, dramatic and impressive, yet it will more than aesthetically enhance the

city through its profusion of accessible retail space and restaurants, transforming the waterfront property

into a vital and exciting gathering place. ■ ■ ■ ■ ■ ■ ■ ■ ■

ABOVE: Situated on some of the most sought-after land in Chicago, the tower reflects the brilliance of the water.
Rendering by Crystal CG, © Skidmore, Owings & Merrill LLP

FACING PAGE LEFT AND RIGHT: Though contemporary in interpretation, the setbacks thoughtfully relate to the existing
architectural vernacular.
Renderings by Crystal CG, © Skidmore, Owings & Merrill LLP

Vista Luxury Condominiums

■ ■

Arzoumanian & Company

■ ■ ■ ■ ■ ■ ■ ■ ■ ■ Once a sleepy bedroom community, the Village of Skokie has kept in step with the times by fostering a booming commercial center and a solid industrial base to complement its diverse residential areas just next door to Lake Michigan and Chicago's affluent North Shore.

Coincident with the addition of the Illinois Science + Technology Park, a major new research and development facility located near Skokie's central business district, the Village began having even bigger ideas about its future. Arzoumanian & Company, a Skokie architectural firm with a long list of residential commissions in the area and a growing portfolio of commercial and institutional projects, was eager to stay a step ahead. In collaboration with Fazan Development, an emerging real estate developer, and Prinmar Corp, an experienced construction management firm, architects

ABOVE: Gracious sky gardens surrounding the penthouse hospitality suite offer sweeping views of Chicago's magnificent skyline, lush landscaping and special amenities including areas for outdoor grilling.
Rendering by Tomasz Zarnowski

FACING PAGE: Vista Luxury Condominiums' forward-leaning design represents mixed-use development on an entirely greater scale for the area surrounding the new Illinois Science + Technology Park.
Rendering by Tomasz Zarnowski

Raffi Arzoumanian, AIA, NCARB, and Joanna Zywczyk, Associate AIA, foresaw even greater possibilities for a 1.3-acre tract in the coming urban transformation occurring around the site of a former auto dealership.

Reaching to the cutting edge of the Village's master plan, Arzoumanian & Company and its partners seized the opportunity to rezone the property to accommodate two 10-story structures with 156 condominium dwellings, 13,000 square feet of ground floor retail space, five levels of parking and a host

of resident amenities. The plan leveraged the property's highly desirable location—literally steps away from both the Tech Park and a new commuter rail station—to sell comfort and convenience to the broadest possible audience: up to 5,000 people projected to work in the new R&D facility, professionals seeking an easy commute downtown, empty-nesters and other active adults who like living within walking distance of Skokie's central business area.

In both form and function, Vista makes a bold, forward-looking statement, especially in a time of transition for the surrounding area. The project's sheer size is textured by an interplay of undulating solids in the façade's contrast of glass and concrete, and strong horizontal lines drawn from the cantilevered appearance of the balconies. Pairs of obtusely angled building edges create a dramatic arch at the main entrance with a distinctively urban flavor. At the same time, the fourth-floor terrace and sky gardens surrounding the penthouse-level hospitality suite—including a multimedia game/leisure room—add desirable amenities for gracious living. ■ ■ ■ ■ ■ ■ ■ ■ ■ ■

ABOVE LEFT: A multimedia/leisure area in the hospitality suite includes spaces for a friendly game of billiards, internet access and big-screen videogames or movies.
Rendering by Tomasz Zarnowski

ABOVE RIGHT: Soaring lobbies create a grand entrance for residents and visitors.
Rendering by Tomasz Zarnowski

FACING PAGE: Just beyond the entrance lobby, the ground-floor reception parlor in each of Vista Condominiums' towers features a fireplace and a magnificent masonry waterfall, creating a warm and inviting space to receive guests or visit with neighbors.
Rendering by Tomasz Zarnowski

X I O

■ ■

Lucien Lagrange Architects

■ ■ ■ ■ ■ ■ ■ ■ ■ ■ Chicago's South Loop, for the last century, has had a slight reputation for troubles—Upton Sinclair's *The Jungle* not the least of the area's less-than-glowing evaluations. But times changed, and as the South Loop transformed for the new millennium, a new market opened up for buildings, but did not demand striking architecture. That is until an old friend of Lucien Lagrange called the architect with an opportunity to build something striking. Lucien soon found himself working on a pair of buildings that extend the intriguing downtown architecture to the South Loop. X I O is not only unparallel in structure, but unparalleled in design.

In the wake of places like Dubai, where new shapes seem to dominate the architecture, the idea for X I O was to have two towers dancing in the sky. They would respond to each other, play against each other. While both towers are skinned in glass and break away from any known form, the two towers are

FACING PAGE: Combined, these two "dancing" towers house 478 units and total more than a million square feet.
Project Design Team: Rachel Branagan, Don Brown, Cayl Hollis, Forest Barruth and James Kemper.
Rendering by Lucien Lagrange Architects

distinctive of one another in not only shape, but also in height: Tower One shoots up 46 floors, while Tower Two hits 33. Because of the slanted shapes of the two towers, virtually all of the condominiums—nearly 500—that fill X I O are distinct. But one consistency is that every unit has a balcony for those great skyline or lake views.

While the architecture alone will bring you here, the designers of X I O really wanted the residents to feel that they are on a permanent vacation at home. The spa is magnificent; it was designed as a cutting-edge, resort-like getaway that features Turkish steam baths, a movement sanctuary and the Aqua Grotto. Even the deck of the spa has a misting park. But the quarter-acre park on the grounds of X I O really ties this futuristic building back to nature for a breather from urbanity. With tall ceilings, high-end appliances, granite and marble countertops, X I O's amenities are themselves a force to be reckoned with.

X I O sits at the edge of the South Loop's Prairie District, which is lined with great, turn-of-the-century Chicagoan homes—including the historic Glessner House—that offer a great contrast to X I O's bold, futuristic design. Just a short distance from the Museum Campus, Grant Park and, of course, Lake Michigan, X I O offered Lucien a chance to put his progressive stamp on an emerging neighborhood, one rooted in the past but looking forward to a new millennium. The simple, bent, glass structures of X I O are a strange and fascinating addition to Chicago, the birthplace of the skyscraper. ▪ ▪ ▪ ▪ ▪ ▪ ▪ ▪ ▪ ▪

TOP LEFT: In addition to its high-rise towers, X I O will feature 10 townhomes over three stories.

BOTTOM LEFT: The towers are connected by a six-story base containing lobbies—a soaring 60-foot space in the north tower—and a large, 12,000-square-foot health club.

FACING PAGE: The fritted, concreted base of X I O meets the townhomes and towers along Prairie Avenue.
Renderings by Lucien Lagrange Architects

CITY BY DESIGN

CHICAGO TEAM

ASSOCIATE PUBLISHER: Michele Sylvestro

GRAPHIC DESIGNER: Emily A. Kattan

EDITOR: Daniel Reid

MANAGING PRODUCTION COORDINATOR: Kristy Randall

HEADQUARTERS TEAM

PUBLISHER: Brian G. Carabet

PUBLISHER: John A. Shand

EXECUTIVE PUBLISHER: Phil Reavis

PUBLICATION & CIRCULATION MANAGER: Lauren B. Castelli

GRAPHIC DESIGNER: Kendall Muellner

GRAPHIC DESIGNER: Paul Strength

MANAGING EDITOR: Rosalie Z. Wilson

EDITOR: Anita M. Kasmar

EDITOR: Jennifer Nelson

EDITOR: Sarah Tangney

EDITOR: Lindsey Wilson

PRODUCTION COORDINATOR: Maylin Medina

PRODUCTION COORDINATOR: Drea Williams

PROJECT COORDINATOR: Laura Greenwood

TRAFFIC COORDINATOR: Brandi Breaux

ADMINISTRATIVE MANAGER: Carol Kendall

CLIENT SUPPORT COORDINATOR: Amanda Mathers

CLIENT SUPPORT COORDINATOR: Christi Simmons

PANACHE PARTNERS, LLC
CORPORATE HEADQUARTERS
1424 Gables Court
Plano, TX 75075
469.246.6060
www.panache.com

Lakeshore East, Loewenberg Architects, LLC, page 110

FEATURED FIRMS

Absolute Architecture PC 20
James A. Kapche, AIA
300 North Michigan Avenue, Fourth Floor
Chicago, IL 60601
312.263.7345
www.absolutearchitecture.com

Antheus Capital, LLC...........................**300**
Eli Ungar
40 North Dean Street
Englewood, NJ 07631
201.541.8003

Arzoumanian & Company **44, 142, 308**
Raffi Arzoumanian, AIA, NCARB
8707 Skokie Boulevard, Suite 204
Skokie, IL 60077
847.763.8707
www.arzoumanianco.com

Booth Hansen **134**
Laurence Booth, FAIA
333 South Des Plaines Street
Chicago, IL 60661
312.869.5000
www.boothhansen.com

Built Form, LLC **78**
Robert Bistry; Arden Freeman; Richard Parks;
Stephen Poston; Michan Walker
311 North Aberdeen, Suite 200C
Chicago, IL 60607
312.738.3835
www.builtformarchitecture.com

Burnidge Cassell Associates...................**258**
Richard C. McCarthy, AIA, LEED AP
Charles H. Burnidge, AIA
25 South Grove Avenue, Suite 500
Elgin, IL 60120
847.695.5840
www.bca-arch.com

Daniel P. Coffey & Associates, Ltd..... **154, 166, 296**
Daniel P. Coffey, FAIA
Sears Tower
233 South Wacker Drive, Suite 5750
Chicago, IL 60606
312.382.9898
www.dpcaltd.com

David Hovey, FAIA Architect, Optima, Inc. **70**
David Hovey, FAIA
630 Vernon
Glencoe, IL 60022
847.835.8400
www.optimaweb.com
Chicago — Phoenix — Scottsdale

David Zeunert & Associates, Inc. **186**
David Zeunert
Richard Twiss
1916 North Fremont Street
Chicago, IL 60614
773.472.4180
www.zeunert-architecture.com

DeStefano and Partners...........................**240**
James R. DeStefano, FAIA, FALA, RIBA;
Scott A. Sarver; Duane L. Sohl, AIA;
Avram Lothan, FAIA, LEED AP;
Mary Ann Van Hook, AIA, LEED AP
445 East Illinois Street, Suite 250
Chicago, IL 60611
312.464.6498
www.destefanoandpartners.com
Chicago — Los Angeles

Epstein..**254**
Mike Damore, AIA
Mark Fischer
600 West Fulton Street
Chicago, IL 60661
312.454.9100
www.epstein-isi.com
Bucharest — Chicago — Los Angeles —
New York — Shenzhen — Warsaw

Ethos Workshop.......................................**150**
Scott Allman, AIA
1112 South Washington Street, Suite 110
Naperville, IL 60540
630.527.6723
www.ethosworkshop.com

Fordham Company.........................**86, 102, 276**
Christopher T. Carley
101 East Erie Street, Suite 960
Chicago, IL 60611
312.587.0900
www.fordhamco.com

Gillespie Design Group...................................**40**
David J. Gillespie
5307 Business Parkway, Suite 101
Ringwood, IL 60072
815.653.7100
www.gillespiedesigngroup.com

Goettsch Partners **56, 162, 246**
James Goettsch, FAIA; Steven M. Nilles, AIA, LEED AP;
James Zheng, AIA; Joseph Dolinar, AIA;
Michael F. Kaufman, AIA, LEED AP;
James E. Prendergast, AIA, LEED AP;
Lawrence C. Weldon, AIA
224 South Michigan Avenue, Floor 17
Chicago, IL 60604
312.356.0600
www.gpchicago.com
Chicago — Shanghai

Goss Pasma Blomquist Architects **182**
Douglas Pasma
Mark Blomquist
1601 Sherman Avenue, Penthouse Suite
Evanston, IL 60201
847.475.1250
www.gosspasma.com

The Hezner Corporation **236**
Kurt E. Hezner
Scott K. Hezner
678 Broadway, Suite 100
Libertyville, IL 60048
847.918.3800
www.hezner.biz

Hirsch Associates LLC **118**
Howard M. Hirsch, AIA; Thomas J. Kane, AIA;
Kevin Pound; Scott Beebe
225 West Hubbard Street, Fifth Floor
Chicago, IL 60654
312.836.0011
www.hirschassociates.com

Integrated Development Group **134**
Matthew K. Phillips
707 Skokie Boulevard, Suite 340
Northbrook, IL 60062
847.480.0700
www.idg-llc.com

Interior Design Associates **134**
Bonnie B. Manson, ASID, IIDA
618 Church Street, Suite 400
Nashville, TN 37219
615.320.7550

Johnson & Lee Architects/Planners, Ltd.........**198**
Phillip Craig Johnson, FAIA
Frank Christopher Lee, FAIA
828 South Wabash Avenue, Suite 210
Chicago, IL 60605
312.663.0225
www.jlarch.net

Joseph Freed and Associates LLC........**178, 280**
Larry Freed
33 South State Street, Suite 400
Chicago, IL 60603
312.675.5500
www.josephfreed.com

Krueck & Sexton Architects **128**
Ronald A. Krueck, FAIA
Mark P. Sexton, FAIA
221 West Erie Street
Chicago, IL 60610
312.787.0056
www.ksarch.com

Kutleša + Hernandez Architects, Inc. **24**
Ivan Kutleša, AIA, NCARB
Manuel C. Hernandez, Associate AIA
1601 South State Street, 5A
Chicago, IL 60616
312.431.9435
www.kharchitects.net

LCM Architects...**192**
Richard A. Lehner, AIA
John H. Catlin, FAIA
Douglas A. Mohnke, AIA
819 South Wabash Avenue, Suite 509
Chicago, IL 60605
312.913.1717
www.lcmarchitects.com

Loewenberg Architects, LLC **110**
James Loewenberg
303 East Wacker Drive, Suite 2750
Chicago, IL 60601
312.440.9600
www.loewenberg.com

Lucien Lagrange Architects.......**28, 98, 114, 312**
Lucien Lagrange
605 North Michigan
Chicago, IL 60611
312.751.7400
www.lucienlagrange.com

McBride Kelley Baurer 158
Keith Criminger, AIA
1417 North Dayton
Chicago, IL 60622
312.266.7400
www.mkbdesign.net

Merchandise Mart Properties, Inc. 262
The Merchandise Mart, Suite 470
Chicago, IL 60654
800.677.6278
www.merchandisemart.com

Mesa Development, LLC 106, 284
Richard A. Hanson
Richard P. Shields
James M. Hanson
205 North Michigan Avenue, Suite 2200
Chicago, IL 60601
312.240.1700
www.mesadevelopmentllc.com

Millennium Park, Inc. 14
Edward K. Uhlir, FAIA
78 East Washington Street
Chicago, IL 60602

Millennium Park
Chicago Department of Cultural Affairs 14
78 East Washington Street
Chicago, IL 60602

Myefski Cook Architects 90, 216
Charles S. Cook, AIA
John W. Myefski, AIA
716 Vernon Avenue
Glencoe, IL 60022
847.835.7081
www.myefskicook.com

Nia Architects, Inc. 138
Anthony Akindele, AIA
1130 South Wabash, Suite 200
Chicago, IL 60605
312.431.9515
www.niaarch.com

Nicholas Clark Architects, Ltd. 82
Peter M. Nicholas, AIA, NCARB
Ann F. Clark
2045 West Grand Avenue
Chicago, IL 60612
312.243.7799
www.nicholasclarkarch.com

OWP/P 220
John Syvertsen, FAIA, LEED AP; Deb Sheehan, ACHE,
LEED AP; Scott Nelson, AIA, ACHA; Jocelyn Stroupe,
IIDA, AAHID; Geoff Walters, AIA; David Bibbs, SE
111 West Washington Street, Suite 2100
Chicago, IL 60602
312.332.9600
www.owpp.com
Chicago — Phoenix

Perkins + Will 94, 174
Ralph Johnson
330 North Wabash, Suite 3600
Chicago, IL 60611
312.755.4737
www.perkinswill.com

Powell/Kleinschmidt, Inc. 186
Robert Kleinschmidt
Richard Twiss
645 North Michigan Avenue, Suite 810
Chicago, IL 60611
312.642.6450
www.powellkleinschmidt.com

PSA-Dewberry 210, 228
Christopher Frye, AIA
343 South Dearborn, Suite 203
Chicago, IL 60604
312.566.9001
www.psadewberry.com
More than 20 locations across the United States

Roszak/ADC 112
Thomas Roszak
1415 Sherman Avenue, Suite 101
Evanston, IL 60201
847.425.7555
www.roszakadc.com

Serena Sturm Architects, Ltd. 266
Martin J. Serena, AIA
William D. Sturm, AIA, LEED AP
401 North Franklin Street, Suite 5E
Chicago, IL 60654
312.595.0370
www.serenasturm.com

Shapiro Associates 36, 60
Architectural Services LLC
Donald Shapiro, AIA
1021 West Adams Street, Suite 400
Chicago, IL 60607
312.421.6004
www.shapiroassoc.com

Site Design Group, Ltd. 52, 170
Ernest C. Wong, ASLA, APA
888 South Michigan Avenue, Suite 1000
Chicago, IL 60605
312.427.7240
www.site-design.com

Skidmore, Owings & Merrill LLP 304
224 South Michigan Avenue, Suite 1000
Chicago, IL 60604
312.554.9090
www.som.com

Solomon Cordwell Buenz 250, 288
John C. Lahey, AIA
Martin F. Wolf, FAIA
Ted Strand, AIA
625 North Michigan Avenue, Suite 800
Chicago, IL 60611
312.896.1100
www.scb.com
Chicago — San Francisco

Stephen Rankin Associates 224
Stephen Rankin, AIA, LEED AP
205 West Wacker Drive, Suite 720
Chicago, IL 60606
312.899.0002
www.srankin.com

Studio Gang Architects 300
Jeanne Gang, AIA
1212 North Ashland Avenue, Suite 212
Chicago, IL 60622
773.384.1212
www.studiogang.net

Techcon Dallas, Inc. 64
Bruce Russo, DBIA
Two Hillcrest Green,
12720 Hillcrest Road, Suite 1050
Dallas, TX 75230
972.788.4005
www.techcondallas.com

TVS Design 204
Michael Hagen
Neale Scotty
Marc Adelman
209 South LaSalle Street, Suite 801
Chicago, IL 60604
312.777.7400
www.tvsa.com
Atlanta — Chicago — Dubai — Shanghai

Valerio Dewalt Train Associates 32
Joseph Valerio, FAIA; Mark Dewalt, AIA; Louis Ray,
AIA; David Jennerjahn, AIA; David Rasche, AIA;
Randy Mattheis, AIA; Bill Kissinger
500 North Dearborn, Suite 900
Chicago, IL 60610
312.332.0363
www.buildordie.com

VOA Associates, Incorporated 48, 198
Michael A. Toolis, AIA, LEED AP
Rick Fawell, AIA, NCARB
224 South Michigan Avenue, Suite 1400
Chicago, IL 60604
312.554.1400
www.voa.com
Beijing — Chicago — Dubai — Highland, IN —
Orlando — Sao Paulo — Seattle — Shanghai —
Washington, D.C.

Walsh Investors, LLC 106, 284
929 West Adams
Chicago, IL 60607
312.563.5400
www.walshgroup.com

Weiss Architects, LLC 292
Steven F. Weiss, FAIA
320 West Ohio Street
Chicago, IL 60610
312.986.1160
www.weissarch.com

W. Steven Gross / Architectural Associates ...232
W. Steven Gross, AIA
2120 North Sheffield
Chicago, IL 60614
773.281.7024
www.wsg-aia.com

Yas Architecture, LLC 146, 270
Stephen Yas, AIA, RIBA
200 South Michigan Avenue, 14th Floor
Chicago, IL 60604
312.786.0500
www.yasarchitecture.com

THE PANACHE COLLECTION

CREATING SPECTACULAR PUBLICATIONS FOR DISCERNING READERS

Dream Homes Series
An Exclusive Showcase of the Finest Architects, Designers and Builders

Carolinas	New Jersey
Chicago	Northern California
Coastal California	Ohio & Pennsylvania
Colorado	Pacific Northwest
Deserts	Philadelphia
Florida	South Florida
Georgia	Southwest
Los Angeles	Tennessee
Metro New York	Texas
Michigan	Washington, D.C.
Minnesota	
New England	

Perspectives on Design Series
Design Philosophies Expressed by Leading Professionals

California	Minnesota
Carolinas	New England
Chicago	New York
Colorado	Pacific Northwest
Florida	Southwest
Georgia	Western Canada
Great Lakes	

Spectacular Wineries Series
A Captivating Tour of Established, Estate and Boutique Wineries

California's Central Coast
Napa Valley
New York
Sonoma County

City by Design Series
An Architectural Perspective

Atlanta
Charlotte
Chicago
Dallas
Denver
Orlando
Phoenix
San Francisco
Texas

Spectacular Homes Series
An Exclusive Showcase of the Finest Interior Designers

California	Metro New York
Carolinas	Ohio & Pennsylvania
Chicago	Pacific Northwest
Colorado	Philadelphia
Florida	South Florida
Georgia	Southwest
Heartland	Tennessee
London	Texas
Michigan	Toronto
Minnesota	Washington, D.C.
New England	Western Canada

Art of Celebration Series
The Making of a Gala

Chicago & the Greater Midwest
Georgia
New England
New York
Philadelphia
South Florida
Southern California
Southwest
Texas
Toronto
Washington, D.C.
Wine Country

Specialty Titles
The Finest in Unique Luxury Lifestyle Publications

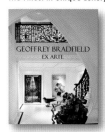

Cloth and Culture: Couture Creations of Ruth E. Funk
Distinguished Inns of North America
Extraordinary Homes California
Geoffrey Bradfield Ex Arte
Into the Earth: A Wine Cave Renaissance
Spectacular Golf of Colorado
Spectacular Golf of Texas
Spectacular Hotels
Spectacular Restaurants of Texas
Visions of Design

PanacheDesign.com
Where the Design Industry's Finest Professionals Gather, Share, and Inspire

PanacheDesign.com overflows with innovative ideas from leading architects, builders, interior designers, and other specialists. A gallery of design photographs and library of advice-oriented articles are among the comprehensive site's offerings.

PANACHE PARTNERS, LLC   1424 GABLES COURT   PLANO, TX 75075   469.246.6060   WWW.PANACHE.COM